The Overnight Family Man

By Paul Guzzo

Aignos Publishing, Inc.

Honolulu, Hawaii
2013

Published in the USA by Aignos Publishing, Inc.
1910 Ala Moana Blvd, #20A
Honolulu, HI 96815
www.aignospublishing.com

Printed in the USA

Edited by Jonathan Marcantoni
Photo by Erika Martin
Cover art by Lisa Figueredo

13-digit ISBN: 978-0-9860233-6-1
10-digit ISBN: 0986023361

Aignos Publishing, Inc.
Honolulu, Hawaii
2013

Also by the Author

The Dark Side of Sunshine

Dedication

To Amy,

Thank you for all you have given to me.

You will forever be the love of my life. I never stop realizing how lucky I am. I love you more each day I am with you.

Paul

Once Upon a Time I Was Single

It was not my finest moment. I was supposed to be lying in bed, naked, with the type of blonde haired- blue-eyed bombshell who most men buy magazines to see naked. Instead, well ... instead I was hiding in her bathroom, writhing in pain.

My genitals burned worse than a sailor's on shore leave in Thailand. I scrubbed my groin with soap as freezing cold shower water poured upon it, but the burning would not stop. I was moaning in agony. The only reason I was not howling like a baby was because Amy, my VERY new girlfriend, was in the bathroom's adjoining bedroom. I figured I already looked foolish enough when I leapt from her bed screaming that I was on fire. I did not want to compound matters by crying, even though all I wanted to do was curl up in a ball and sob until the torture subsided.

I could not picture the evening getting any worse. And then the bathroom door swung open and Amy stood in the opening. I knew I should have locked it! There I stood, my groin lathered in soap, my hand still pressed hard against it - frozen in scrubbing motion. I looked guilty of a crime I was not committing. Now I know how the A-Team felt.

I remained still, unsure how to react. It was already the most embarrassing moment of my life. Before she walked into the bathroom, I wondered how she would ever be able to look at me the same again. Once she caught me soaped up, I figured she would have a hard time making it past that moment. She knew I was not doing what it looked like I was doing, but I was still concerned that the image would stick with her forever and she would know what it WOULD look like if I were doing that thing.

And if the look on her face were any indication, I would soon be doing that thing instead of lying naked with her.

However, luckily (if there is such a thing as luck in that situation), Amy knew why I was in pain and what happened, so rather than accusing me or laughing at me, she sought to help. She thrust a cup of yogurt towards me and said, "Stick your penis in this. It will help."

While she wanted to help, I thought if I thrust my penis into a cup of yogurt what little respect she had left for me would surely go out the window, even if she were the one who wanted me to do it. We were not acquainted enough, I thought, to go on as normal following such an incident.

"No way!" I shouted, gripping my groin and writhing in pain.

"Just do it!" she laughed. "It will soothe it!"

"Leave me alone!" I pled.

"Oh for the love of God," Amy replied and moved toward me. She was actually going to do it! She was going to grab my penis and forcefully stick it in a cup of yogurt. I moved to the corner of the shower and covered up, ready to cry rape if she got any closer.

She finally gave up.

"Fine," she laughed, the comedy of the situation overcoming her annoyance. "If you want to be in pain, then be in pain. If you want the yogurt, here it is." She placed the yogurt on the bathroom counter and left me alone, stifling probably the largest laugh attack in her life until she was out of the room.

What transpired next is something I have never told Amy. When she reads this, it will be news to her – I stuck my penis in the yogurt … and it felt GREAT. Oh my god! It was so soothing. It was the greatest feeling ever. I stood in the bathroom for five minutes with my penis soaking in yogurt.

I thought it was the low point of my sexual life and one that would cost me a great girl.

How did I get to that low point? It's a long story…

It all began with my friend Cephas…

Cephas is an old Jamaican man who runs a restaurant in Tampa. Well, it is not so much a restaurant as it is a lemonade stand that sells food. In the 1990s, an electrical fire gutted the building that housed his restaurant and he did not have insurance to rebuild it, so he instead visited a scrapyard and erected a metal teepee in between his house and former restaurant, which were neighboring structures.

He then built an outdoor kitchen in his backyard and within a few weeks of the fire taking his livelihood he was back in business. In a way, it was the best thing to ever happen to him. People visited his restaurant as much for his personality as they did for his delicious Jamaican cuisine. By working outside, he could talk more casually to people. He then turned his backyard into part of his business, cultivating it to look like a replica of a yard one would see in Jamaica. He built a bamboo gazebo, painted everything the colors of the Jamaican flag, planted mango and avocado trees and started a garden full of vegetables found in his native land.

What people truly know Cephas for, however, is his aloe vera shakes. Most people rub aloe on their skin. He scrapes it fresh from the leaf, mixes it with water and ice and sells the drinks to people. Among its benefits are increased circulation, digestion and fertility in men and women, a lesson I would later learn the hard way.

As a single man, this is where I hung out. I spent hours a day mulling over the world with an old Jamaican guy who sold food and aloe shakes from a makeshift tin hut in front of his house. Not only did be become one of my closest friends, but he also became an advisor to me. I often went to him with my problems and trusted the advice he dispensed upon me.

SO, one day while hanging with Cephas he mentioned that he had a "magical sex rock". He claimed that if you wet the tips of your fingers, ran them along the rock and then rubbed your ... well ... you know ... you would be able to last for hours with a woman. Supposedly, the rock has natural oils on it that would temporarily numb your penis. He said he would never tell women he used the rock, choosing for them to believe he was "Super Man" in bed.

I needed that rock! And he obliged, giving me an extra one. And yes, it was still in the package, unused.

I think that best describes who I was in my pre-Amy days. I was carefree. I was a freelance writer who worked from home and could work when I wanted, wake when I wanted and go to bed when I wanted. My only true responsibility was my dog. I had so few worries that I could spend most of my free time with Cephas and that is the type of place I preferred to be. And I was the type of man who would jump at the chance to use a magical sex rock before I researched anything about it. I never thought life out. I just acted.

A few weeks later softball season began. I had played on the same co-ed team for a few years and we trotted out the identical cast of characters each season. But a few days prior to the first game, one of our female players moved out of Tampa on a whim; we scrambled for a replacement. My roommate's girlfriend found us the player we needed – her best friend, Amy.

It was odd. Amy was my eight-year roommate's best friend yet we had never met. The first game was rained out so our only interaction was small talk in my friend's SUV to and from the field. She sat shotgun and I was in the back. Our conversation was limited to complaining that the game was cancelled

During the second game, we played on opposite sides of the outfield. Our interaction as again limited.

Following the game, the whole team went to a bar around the corner from the field. And that is when the sex rock truly proved it was magical – it brought me love.

A few teammates separated Amy and I at the table, but something about her personality (it of course had nothing to do with the fact that she is hot) allowed me to see right through everyone blocking my way. I could not take my eyes off her and I eavesdropped on every word she said, hoping to find a way to butt into her conversation. I don't remember what spurred the comment, but I remember her saying, "Well, any man not at least engaged, even a broken engagement, before he is 35 is off limits to me – he is either creepy or afraid of commitment." I was 34 ½! I could not allow such a slight to go undefended! Plus, well, she was hot and I wanted to talk to her.

"Hey!" I yelled. "I turn 35 soon."

Without missing a beat, she simply replied, "Then you'll be un-dateable soon."

"Oh, girls will still want to date me," I said with a sly smile. "I have a magical sex rock."

That hooked her. Not because she was looking to have sex with me, but she had to know what the hell I was talking about. I explained what the rock supposedly did and told her all about Cephas and she actually listened to everything I said. Amy is not some hippie chick who looks like she would be into stories about a Jamaican Mr. Miyagi and sex rocks.

She is blonde haired, blue eyed and all American – a high school cheerleader and later a model.

As the night wore on, we found ourselves sitting next to one another, talking like no one else in the world existed. I was shocked this type of girl was interested in me. She later admitted she wasn't so much interested in me at first as she was in learning whatever BS crazy story I had about my magical sex rock, but once we engaged in conversation, she said she felt a natural kinship with me. This shocked her because she said she normally would have avoided long conversations with a guy like me – AKA a weirdo.

I was equally shocked that I was interested in her; I usually dated the type of girl who would not find Cephas odd – hippies. Yet, just as Amy later admitted, I too was drawn to her because it seemed so easy to talk to her; it felt natural. Well, plus, seriously ... she is freaking hot!

There was a spark from the start.

I won't bore you with the details of our courtship except that a few weeks later, on April 23, 2010, we kissed for the first time and when we pulled away Amy said, "Wow." And I said, "We're in trouble." Trouble being this was not going to be a fling. This was real and neither of us was ready for it.

Why weren't we ready for love?

Well, Amy had two children from her previous marriage and her ex-husband was an absentee father, not seen for years. Any man who settled down with her would be more than a stepfather; he would have to become a real father and she did not trust that any man truly wanted that responsibility.

Bringing a new man into her life was a tough decision because it affected her kids, so she had gone out of her way to avoid it. She would date here and there but the dating was simply for fun – going to ballgames, movies, and so on. She never allowed herself to get emotionally involved and if the guy she was dating seemed like he was getting hooked on her she would break it off. She did not want her kids to get attached to a man and then have it not work out. So when we kissed and knew it was "love at first kiss," she was worried. She was not sure how to proceed. And I of course was 34, single and carefree. There was no way I thought I was ready to suddenly take on the responsibility of fatherhood.

So that night we agreed to take it slow.

Two weeks later, we exchanged I Love You's. We couldn't contain our mutual feelings anymore. It was moving anything but slow. However, we both again agreed to try to take it slow from there on out. I would only come to her house when the kids were asleep and if I stayed the night I had to leave before they woke. And While I could hang out during the day with her kids, I could not go to parties or events with them. She did not want them seeing other kids with their fathers and then have them look at me the same. If we did not work out for whatever reason, she did not want her kids losing ANOTHER father figure.

And then ... then the rock came into play.

Despite Amy's early intrigue in the rock, she steadfastly said she would never use it. Not a chance she would state time and time again when I would ask ... no ... when I would BEG her to let me try it. While she was attracted to the odd character (me) who told her about it and she thought it was funny that I had it, it was just too over-the-top for her to actually use. I knew I didn't NEED it (had to say it again for those who missed it), but I was so intrigued by the rock. Did it really work? I had to know.

Then, she finally caved. I did not know why nor did I care. I was so excited ... so excited that I did not learn how I should use it. Cephas had told me but I had forgotten; it had been almost two months since he gave it to me. I probably should have called him or looked it up online. But that has never been my MO. Remember, I just act. I rarely think about the consequences of my actions.

The proper use of the rock is as I stated earlier. Instead, I soaked the rock with water, soaked my ... well ... you know ... and then rubbed the rock directly on it ... all over it.

As we lie in bed ready to test the rock's worth, Amy asked, "Does IT feel any different?"

"Yeah," I said in a whimper as my crotch suddenly felt like it was on fire. "It ... it ... OH MY GOD IT HURTS!"

Minutes later, I was in the bathroom, making love to yogurt rather than my hot ex- model girlfriend.

As I previously wrote, I thought it was a low point in my life, one that would chase away a great girl. Looking back, however, it may have been a high point and the moment that actually won

Amy over.

    Amy was a relationship saboteur. While she was in love with me, because she was not sure if our relationship was in the best interests of her kids, she since admitted she was looking for ANY reason to toss me from her life. The rock incident was more than ANY reason ... it was a BIG reason for most girls to break up with a guy. But when she woke in the morning and realized that not even rubbing a magic sex rock on my groin could dull her love for me, she knew I was the one

    And I always knew it would take a special girl to put up with my eccentric personality. When Amy did not give me the boot following what was undoubtedly the most bizarre stunt I had ever pulled with a girl, I knew she was the one for me.

    It also showed us how well we fill in one another's gaps. The following day, she sent me an email that documented the proper use of the rock. She laughed at how I did exactly what the instructions said NOT to do. This is an example of how we make one another whole – without me, she would never have learned about something as ridiculous as a magical sex rock. My insanity has brought her new experiences. However, her attention to detail helps keep me grounded and safe. If I come up with a crazy idea, she finds out the best way to implement it before I act – she keeps my crotch from catching on fire. When I asked Amy if we could try the rock again she laughed and said absolutely not.

    Following the rock incident, we made our relationship public – there was no turning back. She had kids and if people found out she brought a man into their life she could not rely on as a long-term partner, she would look like a terrible mother. More importantly, it meant we went to events and parties together – the children had a man with them on a regular occasion for the first time in their lives. They began to look at me as a part of their family. I could not abandon them. I jumped into the shallow end headfirst. I was not sure I was ready for children. But I knew I loved Amy and could not lose her. I would find a way to change the man I was if that is what I needed to do for her children.

    Most men would probably have run the other way when they began to fall in love with a woman with two kids. Me? As the rock proved – I act first and worry about the consequences later.

This is why, as Amy has stated, she knew I was the only man for her. This is why she fell in love with me. A man who thinks too much could not handle the situation. And a man who thinks too much would never have proposed to her on October 2, 2010, less than six months after a first kiss, as I did. A man who thinks too much would never have moved in with Amy and her children less than three weeks after the engagement, also as I did. In short, I never think … at all. I'm pretty much an idiot.

The following is a collection of journal entries and Facebook updates I wrote that chronicle my journey from single idiot to family man idiot.

10-22-10
The Puddle and the Ring

It did not look like that much pee. Maybe the translucence of the urine coupled with the clean white floor created an illusion of a shallow puddle. Maybe it was the soft lighting in the kitchen that did it. Or maybe it was because my brain could not imagine that the puddle of urine would be anything but shallow considering the tiny source from which it came.

SO, I figured all I needed was one, maybe two paper towels to clean it up. BOY was I wrong. It was not a shallow puddle of pee. It was an OCEAN of pee! And, when I bent down to wipe it up with my two paper towels, it engulfed my hand. I yanked my hand away, freaked out – this was, after all, the first time my hand had ever gone swimming in a pool of urine – and watched in terror as pee dripped from my fingers.

"I did pee pee in the potty!" said the happy naked 2-year-old girl, the source of this atrocity as she jumped up and down and clapped her hands like a toy wind-up monkey with symbols.

"No, not exactly," I said in hushed terror. "The potty is about six inches to the right of where you peed."

"Stop letting it drip all over the floor! You're only making it worse," laughed Amy.

I simply nodded, still a bit catatonic by the disgustingness of the incident, and ran to the sink, rinsed my hand and proceeded to grab half a roll of paper towels.

Unfortunately, this was still just barely enough to soak up the remains of the watery substance that is the cause of yellow snow up north, and my hand was AGAIN soaked in urine.

"There is your first lesson – don't clean your hands until the job is done," laughed Amy. "And trust me, that is one of the least disgusting things you will have on your hand in the next few years.

"But you know the deal. If you want this," she continued, wiggling her ring finger, "you get some dirty hands."

I nodded. I knew the deal already, but somehow it did not make the fact that my hand smelled like human waste any better.

A few hours later, Amy turned on *Dora the Explorer* (USUALLY the world's GREATEST babysitter… and I stress USUALLY) for her two kids. THINKING this meant we had time to call everyone we knew and tell them the big news, we raced to her bedroom for phone call privacy.

Time to make a phone a call … privacy … HA … Hey, I was a novice! We hadn't left the kids for more than a few minutes before they rushed into the room and jumped onto her bed, screaming that they wanted to watch *Dora* with us and not alone downstairs.

As we lay in bed with the two children between us, watching an episode of *Dora the Explorer* I had already seen 20 times that week, Amy looked over to me with a loving smile.

"You know, it's not too late. You can still take it back," she joked, again wiggling her ring finger. "It's going to be years of dirty fingers and interrupted prayers. This is going to be a BIG adjustment for you. You are sure you are ready for this?"

I looked at the ring on her finger and then to her beautiful smiling face. I then looked to her two kids snuggled up against me as they watched their favorite cartoon.

"I am positive I am NOT ready," I replied. "But I wouldn't give you guys up for anything."

And like that, I became the overnight family man. It is going to be an interesting ride.

10-15-10
Facebook Update
I am tired of moving.

10-27-10
Facebook Update
I am happy to finally have my new house in order ... now to get my old home in order ... I NEED STORAGE! So much stuff that won't fit here ... and a lot of paperwork I don't think should be around kids.

10-28-10
Facebook Update
Oh my god ... I have kids!

10-29-10
Changing My Routine
I am becoming my father. I am becoming annoying.

My father is one of the all-time great dads. Without getting into too much detail, I'll sum up his fatherly skills simply by stating that if a doctor tells me there is a .0000000001 percent chance my heart will give out in 50 years unless I get a new one immediately, I know my father will offer to donate his within an hour of hearing the news. I have a lifetime of memories of my father performing unselfish acts for me to back up that claim.

BUT, while I remember all the unselfish things my father has done for me, I also have vivid boyhood memories of him driving my mother INSANE. All he had to do was ask my mother one question and she would instantly become annoyed. "Aline, am I getting fat?" he would ask. My mother would always snap back, "NO!"

My mother was right. My father was not fat; he was in good shape. Yet, he continued to ask her if he was fat, day after day – Aline, am I getting fat? ... Aline, am I getting fat? ... Aline, am I getting fat? ... Aline, am I getting fat? – and his constant badgering ANNOYED THE HELL OUT OF HER! Why did he annoy her with that question? That is because in my father's mind he was getting fat. While he was in good shape as a father, as a single man he was in phenomenal shape and he must have missed being in that type of shape.

A few years ago, I saw a photo of my father as a 20-something; he was slim and muscular. I didn't even recognize that it was him. When I told that to him, he said, "That is what me minus three kids looked like." I knew what he meant, but I didn't understand him.

Staying in shape has always been a sick obsession for me.

I lift weights five days a week. I play flag football twice a week. I play softball once a week. And I play racquetball as often as I can.

I watch what I eat. I count my carbs. I dine mostly on chicken and fish and a medley of vegetables. I stay away from junk food. I try not to eat past 8 p.m.

I have worked out with 100 degree fevers, migraine headaches, a broken hand and a torn plantar fasciitis.

I have driven through blizzard snowstorms in New Jersey and monsoon rainstorms in Florida in order to get to the gym.

I have always been in great shape.

NOTHING has ever been able to keep me out of the gym ... or so I thought.

I turned 35 last week. Birthdays ceased being big deals for me after I turned 21. I joked for the week leading up to my 35th birthday that I was excited because it meant I could run for president. In reality, though, I didn't care one iota about the day. But when I was leaving for work the morning of my birthday, Amy's son looked at me with sad eyes and asked, "Why are you working on your birthday? You're supposed to have a party and eat cake." I explained that adults don't get days off from work for their birthday, but he didn't understand; he is 4. (I have already learned that simply saying, "He is 4" is all the explanation I need when it comes to explaining his attitude about certain aspects of life.)

Fast forward to 3 p.m.

Amy called me to tell me her son was honestly upset that I was working on my birthday; he wanted to get me a cake and throw me a party. Amy and I had dinner reservations for 7 p.m. My plan was to go to the gym at 5, go home, shower and be ready to leave for dinner by 6:45. Her son's desire to buy me a cake changed those plans. We could not change our reservation, so she asked me if I could be home by 5:30 to have cake with her kids.

I knew I couldn't skip birthday cake with Amy's kids. Her son's desire to buy me cake was not a selfish one; he did not want the cake only so he could eat cake. He really cared that I had a birthday cake. While my birthday meant nothing to me, it apparently meant a lot to her son. Why? Because he is 4, that's why. I didn't have the heart to disappoint him, so I did something that a broken hand, 100 degree fevers and a nuclear war could never convince me to do – I skipped the gym. Worse yet, I skipped it to eat junk food!

And that is when I finally understood what my father meant – kids mean the gym is no longer a right; it is a privilege. Kids mean that eating healthy food is not always an option.

Amy's son picked me out an ice cream cake. It was the type of cake that can give you an instant heart attack if you eat more than one slice; the type of cake that gives you one stomach roll per bite. I did not want any part of it. It looked evil. But the kids were so excited that I had my birthday cake that I knew I had to eat a slice.

When the birthday song was over, I blew out the candles, Amy handed me my slice and I took a big bite. And like that, I took another step towards becoming a real parent. I did what my dad would have done. I put the children's happiness over my own vanity.

A few hours later, following our birthday dinner, the thought of skipping the gym to eat cake still burning in my brain, I confided in Amy that I am afraid of getting fat one day. She laughed off my remark just like my mom used to laugh at my father.
I'm becoming my dad. I know that's a good thing. But it's also a hard thing. And unfortunately, I have a feeling that learning to skip the gym is going to be the easiest lifestyle change with which I will have to deal.

10-31-10
Facebook Update
I am watching Dora instead of NFL pregame... we need to get our second TV installed SOON!

10-31-10
Facebook Update
I experienced my first Halloween with kids tonight ... too easy... that is, if you count dragging two kids in a wagon for three to four miles easy... yeah, easy.

11-5-10
Bad Habit
Baggage Amy brought to the relationship:
1. Two kids
2. An ex-husband/absentee father with whom she has a volatile relationship
3. Ex-laws (her name for her former in-laws.)
4. A 3,500-square-foot house that needed to be packed into our new 2,000-square-foot house.
5. A 70-pound, 2-year-old ultra-hyper dog named Duke.

Baggage I brought into the relationship:
1. Habit, my 17-year-old, 35-pound dog.

Who brought more baggage with them? That answer is easy – ME!

Why is good ol' Habit so much baggage? One simple word can explain that – clingy ... and not just Habit; we are equally clingy.

For 15 years (I bought her when she was 2) Habit has been my shadow. I have lived in three cities, two states, three apartments, two condos and one casita with her. I can count on one hand how many times I slept in my bed in which she was not at my feet. We have taken three walks a day together for all 15 years. I have taken her to parties, to picnics, to bars and to the beach with me. Hell, I have even taken her to work with me. We watch football, baseball, basketball and UFC together.

For 15 years, she has been my faithful sidekick. And it is for that reason that Amy was worried about Habit when we decided to move in together.

Duke could hurt Habit, she said. Also, her kids are 2 and 4 and have only known one other dog in their life, a dog that is large enough to withstand their rough yet innocent play.

They ride Duke like a horse; lovingly pull on his ears, tail and head; and playfully slap him in the head. If they played like this with Habit like this, Amy said, she could easily break. (She is 17 remember and every bit as brittle and broken down as that age sounds.) Or, worst case scenario, they could play too rough with

Habit and, rather than breaking, she bites them.

Amy was also worried about my state of mind if any of the above scenarios played out. She understands my attachment to Habit and was afraid that if something bad happened to Habit because of her kids or dog, I would resent her family. I told her that was ridiculous. I told her I was not nervous about moving Habit in with her family; I honestly was not. And, I told her that if something did happen, I would never resent her family.

I pictured a smooth transition for good ol' Habit and me.

It was not smooth at all.

Habit had a lot of adjusting to do. First of all, Amy is not as big a dog lover as I am so the thought of a dog sleeping in our bed appalled her. She said Habit could sleep on our bedroom floor, but I knew that bothered her too, so I decided that Habit would sleep in her own very expensive dog bed in a separate room.

For the first three days, confused by her new environment, she barked and cried anytime I left her side (Habit, not Amy). At night, her barks and cries were so loud that no one could sleep.

Her barks were not the only problem during our first three days in the new house. All of Amy's fears also came true. Duke did harass Habit and her kids did try to play roughly with her.

I was on edge, lecturing her kids and dog to leave Habit alone. I was afraid to leave Habit's side for even a moment, fearing that if I did she would begin crying and barking, bothering everyone in the house. Compounding matters, Habit has recently begun to pee on the floor, another product of her old age.

All of this created a wedge between Amy and me. Understandably, Amy was beginning to hate Habit become annoyed with me. I grew angry with Amy, believing that she should put up with the one piece of baggage I was bringing into the relationship.

It all came to a boil late at night during our third night together. I decided to sleep on the couch next to Habit's bed, scared if I left her side she would cry and bark and wake up the house.

When Amy discovered me sleeping on the couch, she broke down in tears, stating Habit had hijacked the house. I cried as well, telling Amy that she was right and that I was worried that the only solution to the problem was to get rid of Habit. I was sick to my stomach; devastated by the fact that getting rid of my best friend may be the only option. But I had to. How could I choose my dog over my future wife and step-kids?

But Amy refused to allow me to get rid of Habit. She hates Habit, she admitted, but she loves me, she said, and knows how crushed I would be if I didn't have Habit by my side. She said we would figure out a way to get through the "Habit situation." She suggested that we put a gate in front of the door to the room Habit slept in, keeping her dog from getting to her. We would put pee pads on the floor in Habit's room so she had something on which to pee. We would "gently" remind her kids not to play rough with Habit. And we would give Habit Benadryl to help her sleep at night until she adjusted to sleeping without me (Don't worry dog lovers, Benadryl is safe for dogs).

Amy then went to bed and left me alone with the dog whom, up until three days ago, had brought nothing but joy to my life. I was scared. Despite what Amy said, I knew that if Habit did not shape up the only thing to do was to get rid of her. I could not allow my new family to have to adapt their life to a dog. And, yes, I cried AGAIN. I was going to lose my best friend. When you are 20 years old and buy a dog, you never picture it threatening your pending marriage 15 years later.

I sat next to Habit, my cheeks stained with tears, and begged her to please be good, telling her that I loved her and did not want to get rid of her.

I then went to my bedroom and slept next to Amy ... and for the first time in three days Habit did not bark when I left the room. She did not bark all night. In the morning, there was no pee on the floor. We put up the gate that afternoon, protecting her from Amy's dog (and kids actually) and she happily stayed in her room and slept the day away. We put down pee pads and she used them later that day, not spilling one drop of pee on the floor.

Maybe dogs can understand people and Habit listened to what I said to her.

Maybe what really happened was by day three she realized that this was her new home and her new life and just accepted it.

I really don't care why she shaped up. I'm just happy she did. I am happy I did not have to lose my best friend.

11-6-10
Facebook Update
I hate the door slamming game as much as I hate the toy throwing game.

11-12-10
The Big Move
We were told that we were not ready for what we were doing. Our friends and family were worried.

They were not worried about the quick engagement; they were worried about the move. Married couples who have been together for decades told us how moves almost split them apart. They told us it is one of the most trying experiences for a couple to overcome. How could a six-month old couple survive? Hell, we had to survive not one, but two moves – my house and hers – with two kids and two dogs in tow.

Our first six months together were perfect. They were something out of a love story. A lot of laughs. A lot of fun. A lot of bonding moments. A lot of passion. We bought each other thoughtful presents. She met my dad (She is actually the first woman I ever introduced to either of my parents). We even had the obligatory "make out in the rain" session you see in every cheesy romance movie. Yes, the first six months were perfect.

The romance movie relationship ended during the move. The days were long and strenuous as we packed her 3,500-square-foot house and my 1,200-square-foot condo and crammed it into our 2,000-square-foot house. Some of her furniture took every ounce of strength in my tiny 170-pound frame to carry down a flight of stairs. It took two weeks alone to move her home; we had not even touched mine yet. To compound matters were her kids. The boy would see the mess of unpacked supplies lying around the house and get into them as only a young boy can.

The girl is at the "I think running into the road is funny" phase and every time we opened the door to carry something to the truck she would sprint through the door, forcing us to drop what we were carrying to chase her. It was stressful and it was getting to us.

While packing her stuff, the gravity of the situation also hit us. We were more than merging lives; we were changing our lives. Amy was moving 40 minutes away; the friends she'd leaned on for support for so many years were no longer walking distance away. I was only moving 10 minutes away, but most of my friends are single and childless. As anyone with kids can tell you, my friends might as well be in another country. They are no longer regular parts of my life, meaning I no longer have them to lean on for support. We realized during the move that we are now the only ones on which we have to lean and we realized it during a time that others told us is one of the most trying of any relationship.

And that is what was most difficult about the move. Without friends to lean on during this experience, having to lean on one another for support, for the first time we had to see one another in less than perfect emotional circumstances.

Prior to moving in together, if one of us had a bad day we would push our plans back by an hour or two and have a little alone time while we sorted through our emotional baggage; the other never had to see us in an emotionally-weakened state. We couldn't do that during the move. We were always in one another's face. We could not be perfect for one another at all times.

That is why people usually date for a few years before making the type of leap we made. They slowly but surely learn to rely on one another for emotional support, learning to trust that if their spouse sees them in less than perfect emotional conditions they will still love them. Amy and I never went through that process. We jumped right into the fire. During the tough move, we were both scared to go to the other with our problems, afraid to allow the other to see us vulnerable and emotionally unstable. So, rather than talking with one another, we held it in. We snapped a lot, we argued, we lashed out, burning off the stress we felt from the move through anger rather than talking it out. It was the most stressful two weeks of my life. I did not think we were going to make it. I thought I was going to lose Amy.

I think my father sensed it. At the end of a phone conversation that had to do with anything but the move, he said to me, "I know a move is tough. Remember, as long as you love each other, you will be fine. Just talk to her." I don't know why he felt he had to give me that advice. I never told him we were stressed. I guess parents just know. It was the best advice I ever received.

On November 4, 2010, 16 days after we began moving, we were still not completely settled in. Boxes were everywhere. Electronics were strewn about. It was still hectic. That night, I found Amy sitting outside the house, grinding her teeth, looking frustrated. I asked her what was wrong; to please talk to me.

She said she felt alone. She said she missed her friends. She said without them, she felt like she had no one with whom to talk. I conceded I felt the same way. We spent the next hour discussing all of our fears and reservations about the move and about our future. When we were done, we realized something – the best part about living with someone you love is that they are always there to lean on when times are tough. I know that sounds simple, but it is hard to realize, especially for two people who have only been together for six months.

The move was tough, but we made it.

If you told either of us seven months ago where we would be today, we would have laughed. But we are here and we are making it work because, when all is said and done, we love one another more than either of us ever thought possible.

It's going to be a learning experience, but we will make it.

11-13-10
Facebook Update
I am getting a firsthand look at what happens when a 2-year-old girl realizes the world does not revolve around her ... simply fascinating! I feel like this should be made into one of those Discovery Channel documentaries you see on wildlife.

11-19-10
The Broken Deal
We had a deal dammit! But within half an hour of making the deal, the bowling ball object drooping from inside her pants was proof that she broke it.

Yeah ... that's right ... Amy's 2-year-old daughter pooped her pants and for the first time ever it was my turn to change her.

I know what a lot of you with kids are thinking – "SO

WHAT?!?! So you changed a diaper."

Well, get off your high horses and look at this from my point of view. I did not have the luxury of my first poopy diaper being on a newborn. This was not some cooing baby without a personality. (Sorry, your newborn DID NOT have a personality. You need experiences to have a personality). Amy's daughter is a fully-fledged personality. She walks. She talks. She has likes and dislikes. She has mannerisms and favorite foods and favorite songs and television shows. It is VERY awkward when the first time you are changing a poopy diaper the recipient is capable of having a conversation with you; not to mention the fact that a 2-year-old's poop is MUCH larger than a 2-week olds! Most parents get to build up to a 2-year-old; I was thrown right into it.

Earlier that day I was sitting peacefully in my kitchen, editing an article and watching *SportsCenter* while munching on a bagel. My dog was at my feet. ESPN was on my television. Life was good. Then, it happened… Amy came storming into the kitchen, covered in sweat, looking completely exasperated. She was trying to clean, she said, but every time she got one spot clean her daughter dirtied it just a few moments later.

Please, she begged, take her daughter off her hands for a while so she can clean.

As much as I wanted to help, I had errands to run, I explained. I had to run to the AT&T store and get my phone fixed and then pay some bills that were close to going to collection agencies.

Perfect, she exclaimed, explaining that I could take her daughter with me.

Huh?

It is not that I was worried about spending one-on-one time with her daughter. There are few things I enjoy more than hanging out with her. If someone were to ask me to describe my perfect day, I am not sure how I would spend it but I do know it would include Amy's daughter. In short, I am absolutely whipped on her.

BUT, what worried me was that, for the first time ever, Amy would not be close by when I was alone with her daughter. What would happen if she pooped her pants? (Amy's daughter, not Amy)

Amy, desperate to have the house to herself for a bit (her son was at school), promised me that her daughter had recently pooped so she would not do so again on my watch. I had no reason to believe Amy was lying ... little did I know.

So we were off, Amy's daughter and I, ready to run errands together. I had a backpack full of toys to keep her busy, a fresh cup of apple juice and diapers in case she peed (I had changed a pee pee diaper already, so that did not worry me).

Before we pulled out of the driveway, I turned to her, looked her in the eyes and said, "Look, let's make a deal. You can pee. You can throw a temper tantrum. You can throw toys. You can do anything you want EXCEPT poop your diaper. Got it?"

She nodded her head.

"So what aren't you going to do?" I asked.

"No poop," she stated in an all-too-cute voice.

That is all I needed to hear.

Thirty minutes later we were inside the AT&T store. She was living up to her promise, doing everything BUT pooping her pants. She was running in circles in the store, screaming "WEEEEEEE" at the top of her lungs. She was throwing her toys from one side of the store to the next. She even threw an epic temper tantrum when she store to the next. She even threw an epic temper tantrum when she realized she left her stuffed puppy (her favorite toy) in the car. None of the store employees were bothered by her antics. It was early-afternoon; we were the only two customers in the store and the employees were enjoying watching her; it was pure entertainment.

"Let her do what she wants," said the store manager. "As long as she doesn't break anything, we're fine."

"Well," I rebutted, "she also can't poop her pants. She promised me that she wouldn't, though."

One of the female employees laughed a subtle laugh, and pointed to her pants – the bottom was drooping to the floor like she had just pooped an anvil straight out of a Looney Tunes cartoon (Amy's daughter, not the employee).

"She broke the deal," the female employee snickered.

OH ... MY ... GOD!

The lights went dim ... the walls closed in around me ... the world went mute ... the only thing that existed at that time was me and that big load of poop hanging in that 2-year-old's pants.

I knew what I had to do. I could not call Amy and ask her to come change her daughter. And I could not drive her home to be changed. I had to do it. I had to change a poopy diaper.

I walked up to Amy's daughter and asked, "Did you poop your pants?"

"No," she said, a little shame in her voice as though she remembered our deal.

"Did you poop your pants?" I asked again. "If so, we need to change you. Do you want a clean diaper?"

"Yep!" she said, happy to hear that I would not make her walk around in a poopy diaper. I reached to pick her up, but, before I could, she did the most evil act a 2-year-old with a poopy diaper could do – SHE SAT DOWN!

OH ... MY ... GOD!!!!!!!!!

I grabbed her and pulled her off the floor; I could smell the poop crushed in her diaper. I did not have time to think. I knew if I did I would lose my cool and chicken out and be subject to Amy's wrath. "You kept my daughter in a crushed poopy diaper the entire drive home?!?!" I pictured her yelling.

I rushed her outside and opened the back of the SUV, creating a makeshift changing table. Amy's daughter knew the drill. She held up her legs for me as she had done thousands of times before with her mother, and I tore her pants off. I then took a deep breath and ripped off the diaper.

I am not afraid to admit it – I dry heaved; I gagged. The smell was god awful, like she drank a gallon of milk that day, which I think she may have. And it looked like someone dropped a bowl of pudding in her diaper and then smeared it all over her legs. She then said, "Dirty!" Well, she was right; she was dirty.

I threw the diaper onto the parking lot and poop splattered everywhere. Patrons walking by gagged and scattered in disgust – SERIOUSLY! Amy's daughter, in the meantime, continued to hold her legs and look at me with a cute smile; this was routine for her.

I grabbed the baby wipes and cleaned her up, getting as much poop on my hand as I did the baby wipes, dancing around and shaking my hands, yelling "EWWW EWWW EWWW!!! I HAVE POOPY ON MY HANDS!!!"

Once she was clean, I put a clean diaper on her, dressed her and it was done. I did it. I changed my first poopy diaper.

When I got home and told Amy about my accomplishment, she laughed and admitted that her daughter had not pooped earlier; she set me up! She also said she would be the judge of whether or not I did it right. She undressed her daughter and checked her diaper. She was impressed. She said I did a perfect job. I did so well, she laughed, that she would let me change poopy diapers around the house from then on.

Great ... just great.

11-26-10
Those Who Miss Single Paul

I get the feeling that some of my close friends are not happy for me.

When I announced to everyone that I was engaged, it was received by some of my close friends (not all, but some) with a lukewarm response, a simple "Oh ... wow ... congratulations" in a monotonous, less-than-thrilled tone. At first I chalked it up to surprise, which was understandable. Amy and I had not been dating long and we are both highly private people, so we never made it known to my friends that we were talking about marriage. The announcement was completely out of left field.

BUT, we have now been living together for over a month and some people still seem lukewarm over our pending marriage. Few of my friends have offered to come see our new home. Even more bothersome to me, few of my friends have offered to come meet my soon-to-be step-children. These two children will be a major part of my life from here-on-out. I would think my close friends would want to get to know them sooner or later.

Why the lack of excitement over my life changing pending nuptials? One close friend who originally met my announcement with a "who cares" attitude told me his issue was jealousy.

Let me explain ...

Most of my friends are single and without children and some of these friends want to be married and have children ... desperately. I, on the other hand, never really cared about having a family. Now I could not imagine living a day without Amy and her kids, but prior to meeting them I was indifferent to the whole family thing. My theory was always that if I met the right woman, I would settle down. But, I would never become one of those guys so obsessed with settling down and starting a family that I clung to any woman and ended up in a miserable marriage, which happens to some people. If I ever meet the right woman, I will get married, I would tell people, but if I never meet the right woman, I would further explain, I will never get married.

Amy is proof that my philosophy is right and that good things truly do come to those who wait. Prior to meeting Amy, I dated a great girl – she was attractive and smart and was just a really good person. But I was not in love with her and did not picture myself ever falling in love with her, so I broke up with her. I met Amy just three weeks later and I knew before we ever went on a date that Amy was the one for me. If I had stayed in my previous relationship because I was desperate for a wife, I would not be with Amy today.

Such a dating philosophy did not come without flack. I would always break up with a woman the moment I knew that she was not the woman with whom I would spend my life; I was always worried that if I wasted my time with the wrong woman I could miss the right one. This meant that I was single more than I was dating. Friends secretly (or so they thought) whispered that I was gay. Hell, even my immediate family gossiped about the possibility. For some reason, people had a hard time wrapping their brains around the fact that I did not want to waste my time in a loveless relationship. The gay rumors never bothered me.

First of all, I am not gay (obviously). Second of all, I see no problem with someone being gay; I am not one of those men who think gay is a four-letter word.

And, third of all, I was happy single. Why would I want to be in an unhappy relationship just to appease the peanut gallery?

Some people loved my lifestyle, though. My single friend who recently told me he was jealous explained to me that my single lifestyle made him happy; it meant that he always had a single companion with whom to grab beers and watch sports. More importantly, he said, having a single friend made him feel less awkward for being single. My friend said he believes that many men and women are afraid that they will be the last of their friends to

The Overnight Family Man

settle down. People are afraid of that stigma. But my friend told me that I made him feel safe; as long as I was around that meant he would never be the last single person in the group.

This friend said that when I informed him of my engagement, his first reaction was anger. He said he felt like I was abandoning him and he said my announcement made him feel pathetic. He said he thought, "If Paul Guzzo the single guy is getting married and I have not what does that say about me?" He apologized to me for not being more excited about my engagement and told me that he was truly very happy for me and that he actually knew the first time he saw Amy and me together than we would be together forever. It felt good to hear someone close to me express happiness for me. I wish others would. Perhaps that makes me pathetic, but it is how I feel.

My friend said he believes my single friends who still have not properly congratulated me probably feel the same way as he did.

Maybe my friend is right and my friends are jealous. Maybe they think I don't care if they wish me well. Maybe they are so wrapped up in their own lives that they don't care about my life. Or maybe they are just jerks. Either way, it bothers me.

I don't expect my friends to jump up and down, clapping and screeching in delight and proclaiming that I went to Jared (which I did not). But a simple heartfelt congratulation would feel good.

I have never been happier in my life. I wish others were happy for me.

11-18-10
Facebook Update

I found a new football watching partner today – my soon-to-be stepdaughter. She cheered when I cheered and never cried for me to turn on Dora. Thank god!

12-3-10
The Wal-Mart Experience

"So why aren't we just going to Publix?" I naively asked Amy as we walked towards Wal-Mart, a child in each of our arms. All the items on our list are sold at the Publix around the corner from our home, while Wal-Mart is located 20 minutes away.

Amy simply smiled and said, "You'll see."

Boy would I see.

Ever since we decided to get married, the question on everyone's mind was, of course, how I would handle suddenly having two children. It was even Amy's number one question, to which I always assured her I would be fine.

"I've handled it so far," I bragged to her for the first few weeks we lived together, to which she would reply, "Wal-Mart … Until you've been with the kids to Wal-Mart you don't know what children are truly like."

Whatever, I would think and would simply shrug off the comment. I had no idea how right she was.

We had a simple task ahead of us at Wal-Mart. We needed plug-in air fresheners, dog shampoo and a new doggy gate. Three items. How hard could that be?

Boy what a stupid question.

The moment we entered the store, it began. Amy's daughter wanted to sit inside the shopping cart, not in the cart's child seat. Jealous of her place inside the cart, her son suddenly wanted inside the cart; he was previously walking with us. As soon as he got into the cart, the daughter slapped him in the face. He retaliated by stealing her favorite stuffed puppy and not giving it back. She screamed bloody murder that she wanted it back and again slapped him, this time harder.

He then began to cry in pain. We were only in the store for a few moments and both kids were crying so loudly that even Helen Keller would have been bothered by their presence (yeah, I did it; a Helen Keller joke in 2010!).

BUT, it wasn't too bad. It didn't bother me one bit, I told Amy. I could deal with a little yelling and crying and before Amy could become annoyed with my cocky nonchalant attitude both kids stopped crying and returned to acting like normal kids. No, actually, they were being good, so I guess that means that they were acting like abnormal kids.

I told Amy it looked like I survived my trip to Wal-Mart.

Boy what a stupid comment.

She laughed. "No", she said, "it has only just begun". *I am pretty sure thunder roared outside when she said that.*

We grabbed the air freshener. Only two more items and they

were both in the pet aisle. We were almost done and I was still alive. Little did I know that in order to get to the pet aisle we had to cross the "Parental Aisles of Hell!" *cue the same thunder noise I heard outside the Wal-Mart.*

As we trekked closer and closer to the pet aisle, I noticed that every parent with kids in tow was turning down the bathroom supply aisle. One parent… two parents… three parents... the count kept rising! Why does every parent in Tampa need bathrooms supplies today? I wondered.

Boy did I found out why.

Amy suddenly turned to me and said she remembered that she needed to grab a few other items. She told me to take the kids and she would meet me in the pet aisle. Sounds good to me, I thought. Little did I know, she was setting me up!

It was at that point we split up and my real Wal-Mart experience began.

As I passed by the bathroom supply aisle, I looked down it and found it odd that I saw NO parents with kids there. With all the carts I saw turn down that aisle, I expected to see a disco ball, dancing dogs, old people on trampolines, anything, something amazing that would have drawn so many people down it. But there was nothing. No one was in the aisle. Why? I wondered. Where did everyone go?

Boy would I find out where they went. And I would not find out until it was too late!

It turned out that the parents were just cutting down the aisle so they could go around the aisles directly past the bathroom supply aisle, heading back to the front of the store and looping around to the other side of the store. All that work was simply so they could avoid the next FOUR aisles. If I had known this, I would have followed. But I was an amateur. I had no idea what the other parents were doing, so I cruised right past the bathroom supply aisle and found myself right in the middle of … FOUR AISLES OF TOYS! TOYS! TOYS! OH MY GOD I WAS STUCK IN THE MIDDLE OF FOUR AISLES OF TOYS WITH TWO YOUNG KIDS!!!!!!!!!! OH … MY … GOD!!!!! I NEEDED HELP!!!! HELP!!!!!

Both kids began screaming "I wants" louder and faster than ever before. I hurried past the four aisles and made it to the pet aisle, but it was too late ... Amy's daughter saw a Dora toy! DEAR LORD NOOOOOO!!! NOT DORA!!!

Amy's daughter was in full fledged temper tantrum, screaming and crying like I was trying to dig her heart out of her chest with a dull plastic spork. Her tantrum was so off the charts that Amy's son's case of the "I wants" was quickly silenced, as he looked at his younger sister in complete shock. When a 4-year-old thinks a tantrum has gone too far, it has gone WAAAAAAY to far. In between her crying screams, in a hyperventilating voice, she let the entire store know that SHE WANTED DORA!

If you think it is annoying to read time and time again, then please multiply that annoyance by a ZILLION and you can imagine what the live show was like.

BUT, I would not be defeated! OH NO! There was no way some 2-year-old's Dora tantrum was going to break me!

I lifted her from the cart and placed her on the floor, where she began kicking and screaming, bringing her tantrum to a whole new level. I scooted her near a wall. I stood on one side of her, placed the cart on another side and finished the makeshift cage with Amy's son, forming a perfect square. Then, using my best ringleader voice, I began yelling "Come one, come all and see the amazing tantruming baby! You've never seen anything like it! She will blow your mind!" Everyone who walked by laughed out loud. Fathers winked at me. Even mothers looked like they wanted to high five me! And, yes, I really did do that. This is NOT made up. I figured, if she was going to tantrum, I was going to have fun with it.

A few moments into my show, I saw Amy standing 25 feet away watching, looking half amused and half annoyed by me. She picked up her daughter, calmed her by gently stroking her hair and kissing her, and put her in the cart.

"That is how you calm a screaming 2-year-old," she said. "Not by humiliating her."

"Yeah, but that is not as much fun," I laughed.

"I survived Wal-Mart," I told Amy 10 minutes later as we paid the cashier.

"Yeah, whatever," she said with a laugh.

As we left the store, I could hear the screams of tantruming babies throughout the store.

"Funny," I said, "but I never noticed screams in the store before."

"That's because you usually go to Publix," she explained

We've been back to Wal-Mart a few times since then. And every time is the same. Well, except Amy won't let me perform my ring leader act again. I actually have to calm her daughter the old fashioned way – with love and caring. It worked, but it is not as much fun.

12-10-10
A Very Guzzo Christmas

I have lived a strange life.

I have been mugged FOUR times, almost kicked out of college for terroristic threats on the phone operator (LOOOONG story there), knocked unconscious by falling branches, almost murdered by an angry husband who mistook me for the man who slept with his wife and almost burned my manhood off with a magic sex rock. I could go on and on for thousands of words about the crazy things that have happened to me if I wanted. I have always seemed to find trouble.

Yes, my life has been strange and dangerous.

With such a plethora of bizarre tales, when Amy and I were engaged and living together with her two kids within months of meeting one another, my first thought was, "This is going to get crazy." The equation was there: Lifelong single man with a lifetime of crazy tales + suddenly living with two kids and a fiancée = more wacky tales.

So far I have not been disappointed. Each and every day has been an adventure. BUT, nothing completely outlandish has happened as of yet. I figured this past week would break the seal. We were going to get our Christmas tree!

In every famous comedic Christmas movie there is a zany Christmas tree scene! I knew in my heart that this trip was going to be gold. On the way to buy our tree, the scenarios played over and over in my head.

Perhaps we would have a *Christmas Story*-type evening. We would purchase the tree, tie it to the roof and all would seem as though it was going well. Then, we would shred a tire, forcing me to pull over and put on the spare. Of course, I would ask Amy's 4-year-old son for help, he would drop the lug nuts on the ground, and yell, "Oh fudge!" Only he wouldn't have said "Fudge." He would have said THE word, the big one, the queen-mother of dirty words, the "F-dash-dash-dash" word!

OR, perhaps we would have a *Christmas Vacation*-type evening. We would decide to drive deep into the woods, only to careen around the icy road and barely survive!

We would then cut down our own tree and return home to find that it is the home to forest squirrels. Amy's dog would then chase the squirrels and destroy our home. (Why Amy's dog? My dog is 17; she isn't moving.)

Even better, perhaps when we went to pick out the tree, Amy and I would fall in love with a tall and full tree that we knew would look gorgeous in our living room, but her son would cry that he found a better tree, a tree about which he overheard the employees talking, saying if no one bought it soon they would put it in the chipper. Her son would beg us to save the life of the tree, which turned out to be a Christmas tree right out of a Charlie Brown cartoon. Of course, we would buy the tree anyway and realize how Amy's son filled us all with the spirit of Christmas, or something else just as hokey.

OR, perhaps after we purchased a tree, set it up and went to bed, I would hear a noise in the living room. I would investigate the noise, only to find gremlins running around the home. I would try to fight them off, but to no avail, and the gremlins would murder me with the Christmas tree!

So what did happen? Nothing. We drove to the tree lot without a hitch. The kids were good. We bought a tree with no argument. We drove it home without a problem. We set up the tree and it looked gorgeous. And we all went to bed happy.

In the morning, I told Amy that I was shocked that nothing strange happened. She smiled and said, "Because you have a family now. What you experienced last night was a normal Christmas activity for a family to share. Normal."

Hmmm… a normal Christmas … nothing dangerous or outlandish happening … a FAMILY Christmas… perhaps THAT is the strangest thing to ever happen to me.

12-17-10
Kicked in the Groin

Amy's son and I did not get off to a good start.

Within the first month of us meeting, he let me know exactly how he felt about my constant presence in his home.

The first time Amy and I hung out for two days straight, with a sour look on his face he asked me, "Why are YOU still here?"

When we hit day three, he said to me, "I think you should go home." Yeah, little kids DO NOT mince words.

Over the next few weeks, when it became obvious to him that he could not verbally push me away, he became physical whenever his mother left the room. When Amy was in the room, he acted like he was my best friend, but the second she turned her head to leave he became the devil child! He would slap me in the arms as hard as he could. He would scratch me, pinch me, bite me and spit on me. I ignored his assaults. He is just a little kid, I would rationalize. THEN, he did it … he kicked me as hard as he could in a place you should NEVER, EVER kick a man.

When Amy and I first began dating, she very matter-of-factly told me that no matter how she felt about me, if her son did not like me she could not continue seeing me. This is why I put up with his constant physical abuse; I was afraid if she found out that he did not like me that I would be boarding the first train to Dumpsville. But, when he assaulted my manhood, I had to say something. Amy and I had already exchanged "I love yous." I felt safe enough in our relationship to finally say something. Thank God I was right. She did not dump me. When she learned of his vicious kick, she decided it was time to have a talk with the little man.

She approached her son with the accusations, expecting him to cower or tell her that I was lying. He did neither. He did not deny them or even seem the slightest bit afraid of getting into trouble. Instead, straight faced, he said, "Well, I just want him to go away." OOF! She told him that I was not going anywhere and any further bullying – yeah, she told a 4-year-old he was bullying me – would result in instant punishment.

Following that talk, the aggression became minimal. From time to time he would sneak in a pinch or a slap and even got one more kick in for good measure, but the attacks were few and far between.

Despite flinching whenever he came close to me, I did try to bond with him. He is Amy's son and I wanted him to love me. More importantly, I wanted to love him. But he would not let me in.

The only time he really showed me any affection was when Amy's daughter and I were together. Her daughter and I bonded from the start and when her son saw us showering one another with love he would get jealous of the attention she was receiving and run to me so he could steal it away from her. I would always oblige; anything to try to get closer to him. But we just couldn't click.

I couldn't blame him, though. While he has not seen his father in a few years, he knows his biological father is out there. More importantly, he knows his biological father is not me and he knows I am stealing some of his mother's attention away. Prior to me entering Amy's life, he was the man of the house. He was the only male who received her attention. Then, out of nowhere, some skinny bald man showed up and began hugging and kissing his mother. I understand why he did not like me.

When Amy told him we were getting married, out of nowhere he began to behave better and began respecting me. Amy explained to him that while I was not his father, I was his stepfather, which meant that he had to listen to me. He was not against the idea, but he did not get excited either. He just seemed to accept that I was part of his life. Amy said she thinks it is because deep down inside he wants a father in his life on a regular basis. To be honest, I don't care why he changed, I am just happy that he did.

Once we were moved in together, we began to bond a little bit. I would help him build houses with his Legos and take him on walks with me and my dog, but it was a forced bonding. It was not yet real.

THEN, I took him to the park. Just the two of us.

A few kids his age were in a tree and yelled for him to join them. He wanted to climb it, but he froze. When I asked him why he didn't climb the tree, he told me he didn't know how. Dejected, he then told me he didn't want to be at the park anymore.

On our way home, I bought him a Slurpee and asked him if he wanted me to show him how to climb a tree tomorrow. I had never seen him so excited. He nodded his head repeatedly and yelled, "YES!"

The next afternoon, I lived up to my promise. I took him into our front yard and taught him how to climb a tree. By the end of the day he was climbing higher and higher, so high that I began to get a little worried that he could not get down. He scaled back to the ground easily when it became too dark to see. After only day of tree climbing he was an expert.

Every day for the next week he asked me to take him into the front yard to climb the tree and every day but one (it was raining), I obliged. I loved it. We were finally connecting.

The following week, Amy took him to the park while I was in a meeting. About an hour into my meeting my cell phone beeped, signaling that I had a text message. Amy sent me a photograph of her son in the tree at the park. He looked so excited.

The following evening, I took Amy's son on a walk. Midway through the walk my father called me and we had a five minute conversation. When I hung up, Amy's son asked who that was. I told him it was my father. In the same matter-of-face tone he used just a few months ago to tell me that he did not want me around, he said to me, "You have a father too? I have two fathers."

I would take a lie detector test if need be to prove that he really said that. It was the most touching thing anyone has ever said to me.

That night, we watched football together. He hated it. He thought it was boring. But he watched it anyway because he wanted to spend time with me.

12-24-10
The Naked Truth

The first time I met Amy's daughter she was naked; Amy's daughter, not Amy.

Amy and I had been dating for close to a month and I had still not met her daughter. Amy made it very clear from the start that I was in no way invited to spend the night at her place until she was sure about our relationship. She did not want to confuse her children. Her daughter's bedtime was 7 p.m. Because of work, I never arrived at her house until 8 p.m. I knew she had a daughter because of the dozens of photos of her in the house but I had never actually laid eyes on her. Then came the night of naked somersaults.

She was only 20 months old at the time (Amy's daughter, not Amy) and she was having a "I don't feel like falling asleep tonight" fit. So for the first time she was awake when I arrived at Amy's. She was more than awake, actually; she was full of energy, sprinting at full speed in circles around the second floor of the house, screaming "WEEEEEEEEEE!" at the top of the lungs.

Amy was frustrated with her daughter's late night energy surge. Apparently, she had been running around the house like that all day. I, on the other hand, was new to the show so found it entertaining and amazing that such a young girl could run in circles so fast and not fall over once! I sat down on Amy's bedroom floor and cheered as her daughter continued to run in circles. I even joined in on the "WEEEEEEEEEE!" screaming.

Amy's daughter quickly realized she had a new fan in the house and stopped her impression of Carl Lewis to figure out who I was. She slowly and cautiously approached me, not sure what to make of this man in her home. I introduced myself and told her she might be the fastest baby on the planet. I doubt she understood what I said, so I will guess it was the tone of my voice that made her happy. She jumped up and down and clapped for close to a minute, screaming joyously at the top of her lungs. She even broke into song! Seriously! I have no idea what she was singing, but she was so happy she had to sing! No one had ever been that excited to meet me before! It was awesome.

But, then, it happened. For no reason whatsoever she tore off her clothes! She sat on the floor and pulled off her pajama bottoms.

The Overnight Family Man

Next came the top. And then her diaper! OH MY GOD! NAKED BABY! THERE WAS A NAKED BABY IN THE ROOM! There was a naked baby standing in front of me and I could not have been more uncomfortable. I thought there were rules or laws against me seeing someone else's child naked. My face was beat red and I squirmed around as she stood naked in front of me and babbled baby talk. It was only going to get worse.

She began performing naked somersaults right in front of me! Apparently, it had been a while since a male showered her with attention as I did during her sprinting episode and she was going to continue to show off for me in hopes of garnering more applause. I was simply mortified. With each somersault, a naked baby girl's crotch was being bent towards me. OH MY GOD! NAKED BABY CROTCH! Amy just laughed. She saw how uncomfortable I was and thought it was the funniest sight she had seen in a while.

"She is just a baby!" she exclaimed. "You don't have to feel uncomfortable."

But I did.

As time went on (obviously not much time), Amy and I decided we were ready to spend nights. This meant I had more interaction with her daughter. As I have stated time and time again, her daughter and I quickly bonded. She became my shadow. Actually, she was my naked shadow. If she was in the house, she was naked. She is one of those young children who cries if she has to wear clothes. Her constant nakedness forced me to quickly become comfortable with a naked little girl around me. Within a few months, not only did I no longer flinch when she would perform naked somersaults for me, but I was picking her up and hugging her when she was naked. Prior to meeting Amy, never in my wildest dreams would I have envisioned doing that! I was always uncomfortable simply holding someone else's child. Picking up someone else's naked child would have made me vomit! Yeah, I've come a long way.

Then, when Amy and I moved in together, another naked wrinkled appeared. What if Amy's children saw ME naked? Her children, like most, do not believe in privacy. If Amy is getting changed, they walk in. If Amy is showering, they walk in. If Amy is going to the bathroom, they walk in. And within a day of moving into our new home, their intrusiveness intruded upon my life. Every time I walked into the bathroom, they tried to follow. I told both Amy's children that I think I could go to jail if they see me naked. What is so disturbing is I kind of believed that was true. Her son also believed it to be true and stopped trying to walk in. But her daughter's intrusiveness continued. She would try to walk into the bathroom with me and I would quickly slam the door shut. For the entire duration of my bathroom break, she would cry and bang on the door. She had never been shut out of a bathroom by her mother; she did not understand why I was not allowing her to come in with me.

Then, it happened ... It was just two weeks ago ... I got out of the shower and realized I did not have a towel. Of course, Amy's daughter was standing outside the door, banging on it and crying. Compounding matters even further, Amy was not home! I could not yell to her to bring me a towel!

I scurried about the bathroom, looking for anything to cover myself. All I could find were two wash rags. I spent the next few minutes desperately trying to figure out how I could somehow open the door while holding one of the wash rags over my butt and the other over my front (it was a BIG wash rag ... cue rim shot). I prayed to God, begging him to give me a third hand so I could open the door while holding the rags in place. God did not answer my prayers, though, so my plan was to open the door a crack, cover myself with the two rags, and then open the rest of the door with my foot.

Unfortunately, Amy's daughter was determined to get into that bathroom. As soon as she saw that door open a crack she launched herself at it and busted into the bathroom. I only had enough time to cover my front, leaving my bare butt exposed. She immediately noticed and, with an all time cute voice, she pointed at it and said, "I see your butt" and then walked away.

Guess what? I was not arrested. Apparently it is NOT against the law for a 2-year-old to see your bare butt. But guess what else? I will do whatever it takes to make sure she never sees it or any other naked parts on me again. The only person allowed to see me naked is Amy. I'm not sure why she would want to see me naked, but she does.

12-26-10
Facebook Update

I bought my future stepson a 450-piece Lego set that has a motor that can move your creations. It seemed cool when I got it, and then I realized today that it meant I had to help build everything. Damn ... I'm still a novice at this.

12-31-10
Time

I have a WHOLE LOT to learn.

For a while, I thought I was figuring out this whole parenthood thing.

One of the top questions our friends ask Amy is, "How is Paul suddenly dealing with having to be a father of two?" It is a justifiable question. This time last year my only concerns were myself and my dog, and all I ever had to do in terms of taking care of my dog was toss some food in a bowl twice a day and pick up her poop from a neighbor's yard. Suddenly, I have two children's lives in my hands; the adults into whom they grow will be determined by the job I do as a parent! TALK ABOUT SOME PRESSURE!!!!!!

When asked about my adjustment, Amy always replies, "Paul is handling it well" and she believes that I am. I help with the "child chores," such as bathing them, getting them dressed for the day and for bed, preparing meals, blowing their noses, changing diapers, wiping butts, etc. And when need be I help with the discipline.

At this point in Amy's children's lives, the main issue in terms of discipline is teaching them boundaries and manners. Don't talk back to your mother. Share your toys. Keep your butt in your chair when at the dinner table. Don't climb on the dinner table when you are naked. Normal lessons.

I thought I was doing a decent job. Then I realized that I am not doing the most important thing a father can do – give the children time.

I am busy. To make a good living as a writer I have to hustle. I work on numerous writing jobs a week plus spend time looking for my next jobs. Prior to having two children, in order to complete my daily workload plus life's daily chores – cleaning, cooking, errands, workouts, etc. – I was on the go for 18 hours a day, guilt free. I can't dedicate 18 hours a day to myself anymore. Or, at least not do so guilt free.

I bought Amy's son an awesome Christmas present. He loves to build things, spending hours a day playing with Tinker Toys, Lincoln Logs and LEGOS. He also loves to play with wires. He is only 5, yet knows how to properly connect a tuner, DVD player and television, a feat I still can't accomplish. While surfing the net for toys for children with a passion for erecting things and playing with wires, I found K'NEX, which are LEGO-like blocks that can hook into a motor, allowing creations such as cars and motorcycles to actually drive. TOO COOL!

He exploded with happiness when he opened the present on Christmas morning and immediately grabbed my hand and led me into the toy room to build something. After hours of struggles, we built a crude car that could spin its wheels but was too heavy to move. He was disappointed, but I explained the fun of such a toy is to figure out how to build it correctly and that we would try again tomorrow.

When tomorrow came, the first thing he said in the morning was, "I can't wait to build that car again." All day I was busy. I had to clean the house of the Christmas mess. I then had to get a new cell phone because my old one broke. Then I had to do some work for one of my book projects. All day long, he kept asking, "Can we build that car soon?" And all day long I told him, "Later." Later never came. I was too caught up in my own life and never fulfilled my promise. The last thing he said to me before he closed his eyes for sleep was, "I hope you don't have to work tomorrow so we can play and build that car."

I am not sure how they did it, but my parents always found time for my two siblings and me. We always came first, second and third. Work and errands came a distant fourth and fifth. I could have cleaned on Monday. I could have lasted a few days without my cell phone. I could have worked after he went to bed. My parents would have done any of those three options to find time for their children. But I didn't. I thought of myself first. And I am sad to say that this is one of a few similar occurrences. I am struggling to remember to put the children first. Actually, a good father doesn't have to remember. It comes natural.

I feel like the biggest jerk in the world. I feel like a terrible father. No, I am a terrible father. To make matters worse, Amy thinks I am a great father, while in reality I am the exact opposite.

I have so much to learn.

1-14-11
It Was NOT Awesome Baby!
I'm a guy.

While I am not the world's biggest college basketball fan, because I am a guy, by law I have to at least follow the standings, keep up with what teams are good, and watch a handful of games a season. If I don't and I am at a bar one night when a college basketball debate breaks out and cannot intelligently add to the conversation, by law the other men in the bar debate are allowed to castrate me, smear my face with makeup and call me Judy. I swear! It's law!

So, while I don't watch college basketball fanatically, I watch it casually, which is enough for any man to become a big time Dick Vitale fan. Surely you know who Dick Vitale is! He is THE voice of college basketball! If you click on ESPN for just a few seconds during a game he is announcing, his voice is the one rattling your chandeliers. He is the chrome-domed, over the top, mega-excited color commentator who has coined such phrases as:

"It's awesome baby with a capital A!"

"He's a real diaper dandy baby!"

"He's a PTPer baby!"

"It's awesome baby with a capital exclamation point!"

He is a living legend in the sports world. And, just a few weeks ago, I had the opportunity to interview him for an article. To say I was fired up would be an understatement. I called every guy I knew and bragged about the opportunity. I was on top of the world!

There was one issue ... Because of his ESPN duties, he was on the other side of the country. The interview would have to be done by phone and I did not know when he would be calling me. I was informed that I needed to keep my tape recorder and notepad on me at all times for the next 24 hours because he would call me whenever he had 30 minutes free. In the past, this would not have been an issue. I have performed numerous interviews under such circumstances. In the past, though, I did not have two kids.

Amy was sick that day. She was laid up in bed, leaving me in charge of two hyper kids. I did ok for most of the day. I took them to the park so that Amy could get a few hours of silence. I sat down with them and watched a movie to calm them. I felt like an old pro! Then, dinnertime arrived. Oh boy. They were hungry. They were in that screaming, "I am hungry" mode! A true old pro would have realized that there was no way to cook for two screaming hungry kids and taken them out for pizza. While I may feel like an old pro at times, I am really a novice. I decided to cook. Worse yet, I decided to be the hero and cook their favorite meal – Macaroni and cheese with sides of broccoli and garlic bread. I envisioned a Bill Cosby moment, the two kids dancing around the kitchen singing, "Paul is great, he gives us mac and cheese!"

Unfortunately, they did not sing, nor did they dance. Instead, they acted like REAL kids ... they fought. Amy's son was playing with a napkin. Amy's daughter was jealous that he had a napkin. Rather than asking me for a napkin of her own, she grabbed it from his hand, tearing it and starting WWIII. They were at each other's throats, screaming, crying, pushing and even biting! Yes, this was all over a napkin. A NAPKIN!!!!

Things got worse. As I tried to break it up and discipline them, the water began to boil over! Then, my phone rang. I'm sure you know who it was ... Dickie V.

I had to answer the phone. I tried to talk to Dick Vitale and ask if I could call him back, but the screaming kids were too loud. I couldn't break up the fight because I had one hand on my phone and the other was pulling the pot of boiling water off the burner. Then, yes THEN, it got even worse!

Anytime a house gets loud, dogs always have to get add to the noise. It must be in their contract. My dog began barking and Amy's dog began leaping at the door that separates the dog room from the kitchen. BARK BARK ... BANG BANG ... BARK BARK ... BANG BANG! It was getting ridiculous ... and it then got EVEN WORSE!

My phone reception began to weaken. I HATE AT&T!

Let me review the situation: Water is boiling over. Kids are screaming. Dogs are barking and slamming into doors. Reception is weak. And I have Dick Vitale on the phone. Oh yeah, and he is in his car; the roar of the road and his engine were adding more noise!

He is yelling, "Hello? PAUL? Is this Paul Guzzo? Do I have the right number?"

And I am yelling, "Mr. Vitale! I have two screaming kids, water boiling on the stove, a bad reception, dogs going crazy and a sick fiancée! Can I call you back?!"

The louder I screamed, though, the louder the kids screamed and the louder the dogs became! With the bad reception and the noise, I think all he heard was, "Mr. Vitale ... I have two kids ... boiling on the stove ... and a bad, crazy ... fiancée!"

This went on for 30 seconds. He kept asking if he had the right number and I kept screaming that I needed to call him back. And then ... click. He either hung up or AT&T dropped my call. I looked at caller ID on my phone and my heart sank. He called from a private number. I could not call him back. I lost my interview with Dick Vitale.

Oh, of course this story has a happy ending! He called me back the next day! He told me he tried to call me the night before but thinks he might have called the wrong number because all he heard was static and yelling. I told him he must have dialed the wrong number because I never received a call and I did not see any missed calls on my caller ID.

A few minutes into the interview, as we discussed our families, he asked if I had any children. I have two step-kids, I told him, and they are perfect angels.

1-22-11
Facebook Update
I am really getting skinny ... I am beginning to look like those kids that fat woman from *All In The Family* looks after. Seriously, flies are beginning to stick to my eyelids. I think I need to change gyms. Mine is only open until 9 p.m. and I am beginning to realize that the only time I can go to the gym is after 9 p.m.

1-28-11
A Sobering Experience

Guess what? The Gasparilla Parade actually has floats ... incredible floats! And the people who take part in the parade have equally incredible costumes.

I've been going to the parade for 11 years and this past weekend was the first time I ever noticed that there was a parade.

Yeah, you guessed it. I went to the Gasparilla Children's Parade, which is an alcohol-free version of the regular Gasparilla Parade – Tampa's Mardi Gras. For the first time since I was a little kid, I watched a parade without any alcohol in my system. It was truly a one-of-a-kind experience.

The adult version of the Gasparilla Parade, held one week after the children's parade, is not about the parade. The city can try to force feed the public that the grand tradition revolves around the krewes and the floats and the spectacle of it all. But we all know the truth. Gasparilla is about waking up at the crack of dawn, opening a beer or pouring a stiff drink, and keeping the party going until the sun rises the following day. There is nothing wrong with having such an agenda. We all work hard for 364 days a year. One day a year of pure drunken revelry is good for the soul. If you don't believe me, just look at the type of people who are against drinking at the Gasparilla Parade. Who looks happier, those at the parade or those poor judgmental souls who stay home on parade day.

Being sober for a parade had its drawbacks. Normally, the bitter cold on Gasparilla doesn't bother me. The whiskey keeps me warm. The children's parade was freezing! The bathroom lines at the Children's Parade are just as bad. Children take an hour to pee and there was no way I was going to pee at my normal Gasparilla Parade spot – in the alley behind that giant white house near the corner of Swann and Bayshore. (Yeah, I pee in your alley every year Daddy Warbucks! DEAL WITH IT!) And being sober made it tougher to deal with the parade jerks. Yes, people were being jerks at a children's parade. I actually saw adults jumping in front of kids for beads.

But, the positives did outnumber the negatives. I will admit I realized this weekend that my desire to be a heathen has caused me to miss almost a dozen years of fine parades. I honestly never watched more than a few minutes of the parade a year since I moved to Tampa. My friends and I would usually stumble to the parade route late morning/early afternoon, find a good spot to camp at for the next few hours, and have our backs turned to the parade as we mingled with the hundreds of thousands of other parade goers crammed into the parade route.

Actually standing calmly and watching the parade was a great experience. For the first time ever, I appreciated the work the krewes put into their floats and their costumes.

More importantly, I appreciated how much fun parades used to be before they became all about getting drunk and blowing off steam. I was smiling ear-to-ear all day as Amy's son jumped for joy every time he acquired more beads and as her daughter danced to every song blaring from each float's speakers. This was their first true parade experience (school parades on the playground with only the parents as spectators does not count) and they soaked in every second of it. The temperature was freezing and the parade was over three hours long, but they could have watched the floats, chased after beads and danced for another three. It was awesome to watch.

I was told by most of my friends who have children that one of the best parts of being a parent is that you get to experience everything for the first time again. The best example they gave me was Christmas. They explained that Christmas loses its luster at some point in our lives; it just becomes a day when we exchange presents. But, once you have kids, it becomes exciting again as you watch them gleefully tear wrapping paper off boxes and jump for joy when they realize they received the presents they desperately wanted. My friends were right. Christmas was fun. In fact, the children have made a lot about life fun again – climbing trees, walks in the park, watching airplanes take off, cartoons, fireworks, playing with Lincoln Logs and Tinker Toys and Legos, and so on and so on! I get excited just writing about it! And in the years to come I have picnics, baseball games, riding bikes, fishing, camping, and so much more! I'm beginning to realize that I am getting more out of the children than they are getting out of me. They have provided me with a second lease on life.

With all that said, I can still enjoy a good adult beverage every once in a while. I will be attending the adult Gasparilla Parade this weekend. I will be a heathen for a day. I will probably NOT watch the parade. And I will probably pee in that same alley. Try and stop me Daddy Warbucks! Just try!

2-4-11
An Even MORE Sobering Experience
According to my Uncle Joe, my father used to be cool.

He dropped this bombshell on me at my sister's wedding a few years ago.

Apparently, my father, my uncle and a group of their cousins and uncles all owned land in Vermont with a cabin. Each year, they all trekked up to Vermont for a week of fishing, hunting and general male debauchery. While my uncle conceded that my father rarely partook in the excessive drinking, he said my father never missed the annual trip and always had fun ... until my older sister, younger brother and I were born. Then, said my uncle, my father continued to go for a few years, but stopped having fun. Instead, all he talked about was having to get into town to find a pay phone so he could call home and check on his wife and kids.

According to my uncle, my father's final trip to Vermont ended after only two days. From the time they arrived in Vermont that year, my father was looking for a reason to go home early to see his family. When the weather called for rain for a few days, my father said it looked like it would be a wasted trip so perhaps he would go home. When they had trouble getting the fire stove started, my father said that if the cabin was going to be too cold he would go home. This continued for two days, until my Uncle Cliff came down with a stomach bug and needed to go home to see a doctor. My father jumped at the opportunity. He told Uncle Cliff he would drive him home and then just return home himself.

The trips to Vermont remained an annual tradition for the other men, but my father was no longer a part of that tradition.

My father could not stand to be away from his family.

"Your father got old," laughed my uncle at the conclusion of his tale.

Gasparilla is my annual tradition. Eleven Gasparillas have come and gone and I have partaken in each. Every year I woke up at 8 a.m., jumped in the shower, chugged a gallon of coffee, cracked a

The Overnight Family Man

beer and walked outside. My neighbors would stumble from their homes one by one, each holding a drink of their own, each inviting me into their home to sample their brew – Mimosas, Screwdrivers, Bloody Mary's, and so on.

Around 10 a.m., I would then fill a backpack full of beer and hike from my Harbour Island home to the bridge so I could watch the pirate invasion. Then, I would travel with my posse of friends to our regular spot under the Davis Islands Bridge, pretend to watch the parade, chug beers, catch beads and urinate in the alley behind that giant white house near the corner of Swann and Bayshore, all before taking the few mile walk to Hyde Park, where we continued the party at the many bars that line Howard Avenue. Each year was the same. And each year I had a ball.

Then, I became an overnight family man.

Amy did not have problem with me attending Gasparilla this year. She actually thought it was a good idea. I made the transition from single man to family man so quickly that she thought a day of partying with my single friends would be good for my soul; it would be a good way to blow off the stress that comes with family life. I agreed, of course. What man would argue against his significant other's opinion that a day of drinking is a good thing?

I slept at my brother's Harbour Island home the night before the parade so I could get an early start as I did every year. I woke up at 8 a.m., showered, chugged some coffee and cracked a beer. I walked outside and saw the neighbors filing from their homes, offering their beverages to the neighborhood … And then I called Amy to tell her and the kids good morning. I stayed on the phone with them for 20 minutes while the rest of the neighborhood partied.

I finally joined the celebration, but stepped away every five minutes to text Amy. "How do you feel today?" "Are the kids ok?" "Are you having trouble getting cell phone connection today because of the number of people in downtown Tampa for the parade?" "Do you have food? It will be hard to get to the store today." And so on.

After each text, I would send another saying, "If you need me to come home, I will. I don't need to be at the parade." I was searching for an excuse to go home. I was miserable. I missed them. I had not been away from them for an entire day since we all moved in together. I promised Amy I would not drive home that night because I would be drinking and I forbid her from picking me up because of all the drunk drivers on the road. If I attended the parade, I would not see her for an entire day. It sounded terrible.

She kept texting me back: "No, we are ok. Have fun."

I could not have fun.

I only drank the one beer that morning. I was worried that I would get drunk and then get a call from Amy saying there was an emergency. If I was drunk, I would not be able to help. I turned down beers, mixed drinks and shots.

I tried to have fun. I really did try.

Following the morning festivities, I made the annual journey to the Harbour Island Bridge to watch the invasion. I still did not have fun. All I thought about was how much fun Amy and the kids would have had watching the pirate ship dock.

I then went to our regular spot under the Davis Islands Bridge and waited for the parade to start. Everyone was in high gear – chugging drinks, screaming "woo!" and mingling with a few hundred thousand of their closest friends. And I still was not having fun.

I saw two kids having a sword fight with Styrofoam pirate swords and became fixated on their game, imagining Amy's kids playing a similar game. Then, someone jolted me to attention by slapping me on the back and asking if I wanted a beer.

"No," I said. "I want to go home."

And I did.

I walked off the parade route and journeyed by foot five miles home, only stopping for a moment to pee in the alley behind that giant white house near the corner of Swann and Bayshore.

When I burst through the door of our home, Amy laughed at me. She said I could have stayed at the parade all day and had fun.

"I'll have more fun here," I said. And I did.

We sat on the couch and watched movies as hundreds of thousands of people partied like it was 1999.

That reference makes me old.

Skipping the parade does not.

Skipping the parade means I am truly an overnight family man.

I love my family more than I love Gasparilla.

2-11-11
Meet the Ex-Laws

I gained more than a fiancée. I gained more than two children. And I gained more than a new dog. I also gained ex-laws.

"Ex-laws" is the term Amy uses to describe her ex-father, mother and sister-in-law. She may be divorced, but because they are her children's grandparents and aunt, they are forever part of her family, which means they are also now forever part of my family.

Amy is more than accommodating to them. Despite her contentious relationship with her ex-husband and despite the fact he does not help her raise the children, she treats her ex-laws with nothing but respect. They defend their son and his actions, often resulting in moments that cause her extreme stress, yet she does not take it out on them. Her children adore them; they make her children happy, and that is all that matters to her. She allows her children to talk to them on the phone for hours a day. And, prior to us living together, she always allowed them to spend the weekend at her home whenever they were in town so that they could spend every minute of their visit with their grandchildren. For most, this would be awkward. The parents of your ex-husband staying at your home is not normal. A lot of women would never agree to such a temporary living arrangement. Then again, Amy is not most women. After all, she can tolerate me.

The first time I met them was during her daughter's second birthday party. Amy and I were not yet engaged nor were we living together, but we were obviously more than a dating couple. It was apparent to anyone who saw us together that we were permanent, which made meeting her ex-laws so damn awkward. It was different than meeting future in-laws. Future in-laws only care if you are worthy of marrying their daughter. The ex-laws were judging me on whether or not I was worthy of raising their grandchildren, their son's children. The pressure was on me to impress.

I was nervous. Real nervous. I arrived at the party early to help Amy set up and they were of course there; it was their home for the weekend. Moments after I arrived Amy had to dash off to take care of some pre-party details around the home. The only other people there were her ex-law I had just arrived and would have to confront them already.

They were sitting in the den, watching *Dora the Explorer* with the children. This was awkward moment number one. Amy and I had only been together for a few months at the time, but I had already grown close enough to the children that I would greet them each with a big bear hug. I was not sure how to greet them in front of their grandparents. I was not sure if they would think it was appropriate for a man Amy was dating to be so close to the children already. They knew nothing about me. For all they knew, I was just some scumbag who was using their grandchildren's affection to get to Amy.

I did not have to decide whether or not I should hug the kids. When Amy's children saw me, they rushed to me and hugged me, which led to awkward moment number two. Amy's daughter did not know many words at the time, but one that she did know was "Pepa." Pepa is what she has always called her grandfather. And, for some reason, it is what she has always called me. When she hugged me, she repeatedly yelled in an excited tone, "Pepa! Pepa!" I was not sure how to react. Here I was, a complete stranger to Amy's ex-laws, hugging their granddaughter and stealing a term of endearment once used to describe the grandfather only.

Then, came awkward moment number three. Amy's son introduced me. "This is Paul," he happily told them. "He plays catch with me!" That was our new activity. I had just recently purchased him a Velcro baseball glove and a tennis ball to make it easier for him to catch. Prior to the Velcro glove, he hated having a catch because he had not yet developed the necessary hand-eye coordination. The Velcro glove made it easier and he fell in love with the game. Though I am sure they were happy to see their grandson fall in love with a sport, I figured they must have also been fuming inside. Having a catch with their grandson is something the father, their son, should be doing, not some bald skinny guy who has no blood relation to him.

And then came awkward moment number four…

Once the introductions were complete, we were stuck staring at each other, wondering what to say. I am rarely at a loss for words. You could drop me off in the middle of China with no English-speaking individuals around for miles and I could find something about which to talk, such as Chinese food, Chinese checkers,

Chinese boxing or the unification of the Chinese Proper in 221 B.C., a time that saw the western frontier state of Qin subjugate its remaining rivals.

I drew a blank when it came to the ex-laws. The only thing that I knew we had in common was the kids, but I felt that telling stories about the children and me would only rub salt in their wounds; it would seem like I was yelling, "I am helping to raise your son's children!" I decided to stay away from that.

I stood in the den silently. They sat silently. It was outrageously awkward for a good minute. Then, I remembered something we had in common. They are Mets fans!

Bingo!

"So," I stammered, "do you think the Mets will FINALLY fire Omar Minaya."

Amy's ex-father-in-law's eyes lit up.

"I sure hope so," he said.

For the next five minutes, we discussed the Mets and their current state of disarray. Then, Amy showed back up. She looked shocked that we were having a pleasant conversation. To be honest, I think we all were.

Never one to overstay my welcome, I took advantage of Amy's reappearance and offered to help her set up for the party.

Throughout the course of the party, I crossed paths with the ex-laws on a number of occasions and we shared a few more moments of small talk.

After the party, Amy, one of her friends and I were outside, away from the ears of her visiting ex-laws. Amy was still stunned at the pleasant way her ex-laws and I got along.

"Actually," chimes in her friend, "they came up to me and told me that Paul seemed like a really good guy."

Well, of course they did, I thought. I am an awesome guy!

In retrospect, I think they were as nervous to meet me as I was to meet them. I think that the simple fact that I started the conversation with them and was pleasant to them even though their son is unpleasant to Amy showed them a lot about my character. Plus, let's be honest – I rock; it is impossible not to love me!

Today, our relationship is basically the same as it was at the party. When they visit the grandchildren at Amy and my home, we exchange pleasantries and a little small talk. We don't have a spare bedroom for them, so they cannot spend the weekend at our home. Amy and I do, however, leave our home for a few hours so they can spend alone time with the grandchildren. Yes, I allow Amy's ex-laws to take over my home for a few hours. Is that normal? Probably not. But neither is the family that Amy and I have started.

This is the 21st century after all. Norman Rockwell is dead.

2-18-11
A Major League Decision
I've been thinking a lot about baseball recently.

I am a Mets fan, as is Amy's ex's side of the family. Naturally, this would mean that Amy's 5-year-old son will gravitate towards the Mets. In theory, this sounds fantastic. In theory, picturing him sitting next to me on the couch every night cheering for the Mets sounds very Rockwellian … in theory.

Part of me feels guilty for wanting him to cheer for the Mets. Part of me feels selfish. Part of me thinks my desire for him to be a Mets fan is only fed by my desire to create that picturesque family moment of father and son attending ball games together wearing matching jerseys, high fiving one another during key moments in the game, and watching his eyes light up as I buy him a giant tub of popcorn. My father-son fantasy is also where the problem lies. We live in Tampa, not New York. If he is a Mets fan, he will rarely be able to enjoy the sensation of attending a baseball stadium jam packed with tens of thousands of other fans cheering for the same team. He will never know the instant camaraderie you experience with the fans in your section, simply based on the fact that you all cheer for the same team.

True, I can take him to New York for a game once a year, but it is not the same as attending multiple games a year. And attending games is not the only part of baseball he would miss out on if he became a Mets fan. There is also the fun of following your team in the newspaper every day, memorizing the box scores and your favorite players' statistics, and looking forward to downtime in school each day so you can discuss the team with your friends, all of whom cheer for the same team because it is the local team.

I know that there are so many more important matters for me

The Overnight Family Man

to focus on as a parent, yet this one seems to be near the top of my list. Do I raise him to be a Rays fan so he can experience the fun of being a hometown fan or do I raise him to be a Mets fan so I have someone with whom to cheer along? Or, do I bight the bullet and, GASP, become a Rays fan so I get the best of both worlds?

Why is this an issue with me? Because one of my primary concerns with Amy's son is forming a strong bond with him.

We are having an easy time bonding now. All I have to do is take him on a walk, help him climb a tree, build Tinker Toys and Lincoln Logs structures with him, and occasionally take him on trolley rides or to the arcade and he brags me up to everyone as his best friend. But, he is only 5-years-old right now and his real father is not in the picture. What is going to happen when his father returns and he is older, realizing I am simply a man married to his mother, not his father? I am bracing myself for the day he screams at me, "You're not my real father!" I am bracing myself for the clashes we are certain to experience. All fathers and sons clash when the son hits his teens. It is part of the boy's growth process; he wants to prove he is his own man and no longer a little boy, so he fights for his independence. But, most fathers and sons make it through this tenuous time because they have that true father-son bond; they are blood. We will not have that bond.

When I went through that "seeking my independence" stage, the one thing that kept my father and I on friendly terms during even my worst behaved days was sports. We are both sports junkies and no matter how turbulent things became, we would always find ourselves sitting in the same room late that night watching whatever sport was in season. No matter how irrationally angry I became with my father, if he had tickets to a Mets game the following day we would attend the game and have a ball, as though the argument never happened.

My father was not a Mets fan; he was a Pittsburg Pirates fan. I began following the Mets in the early 80s due the simple fact that they were the best team in the league. I was a little kid; bandwagon-jumping is acceptable at that age. Though my father was not a Mets fan, he took me to multiple Mets games a year. He was, IS, that good of a father.

Part of me will be forever angry that my father and I cheered for different teams. We never experienced that moment of bliss when a team we shared in common won a title. However, we did not need it to keep us close. Part of me wonders if Amy's son and I will need that moment, that bond to get us through the tough times that lay ahead.

Amy continually reassures me that her son will forever look at me as a father figure. His real father is not raising him. I am. But I am also the man who has to discipline him. When his real father resurfaces, he will be a weekend dad at best. Weekend dads buy presents; they don't discipline. At some moment, his real dad will become the "cool and fun dad" and I will just be the jerk who sends him to his room. But, if we share a common sports team, perhaps that will help us to remain close.

I love her son. He calls me his best friend at least once a day and that title means more to me than anything else in this world.

I don't want to lose that title.

Perhaps the Mets or Rays can help. I just have to figure out which to team it will be.

2-24-11
Facebook Update
Life is about to change ... AGAIN ... and in a BIGGER way. Yes, it is possible. Stay tuned!

2-25-11
The BIG Announcement
The older I get, the more I realize that perhaps the most profound quote ever written or spoken came from the pen of John Hughes and from the mouth of Matthew Broderick as Ferris Bueller: "Life moves pretty fast. If you don't stop and look around once in a while, you could miss it."

Life has moved pretty fast for me over the past 10 months and two days. (Yes, I am that guy. I know exactly how many days Amy and I have been together.)

A year ago, I worked 18 hours a day and could do so with no guilt. My only responsibilities were walking my dog twice a day and playing flag football and softball.

A year ago, I could sleep in whenever I wanted or lay on the

The Overnight Family Man

couch and watch the same episode of Sports Center four or five straight times.

A year ago, I never had to miss a major sporting event on television to watch *Dora the Explorer.*

A year ago, Friday and Saturday nights at the bar were the norm; they were expected.

A year ago, I did not need to check if a baby sitter was available before I made plans.

A year ago, I could eat junk food on my couch whenever I wanted. I never had to worry about setting a bad example for kids.

A year ago, I could curse like a sailor around my home without a twinge of guilt.

A year ago, I never had to worry about someone busting into the bathroom as I sat on my throne, asking me if I could play with them when I was done.

A year ago, I had no idea that Wal-Mart could be such a scary place to visit.

A year ago, I could honestly say that someone else's poop or pee had never touched my hands and that I had never wiped anyone's butt except my own.

A year ago, I never skipped the gym.

A year ago, my dog was not a problem. There was no one in my home tugging on her ears or pulling her tail I feared she would bite.

A year ago, a life in the suburbs was a laughable notion to me.

A year ago, my name was synonymous in my circle of friends with the phrase "single for life."

A year ago, climbing a tree was not regular activity.

A year ago, waking up at 8 a.m. to watch tee ball was laughable.

A year ago, a Christmas Tree seemed like a silly expense.

A year ago, Gasparilla was my Christmas morning.

A year ago, I had no idea what an "ex-law" was.

A year ago, my only concern was myself.

A year ago, I told people I didn't care if I ever got married or had kids and I meant it.

Today, I live with my wife-to-be and my two step-children-to-be. Life has certainly changed and changed FAST.

Some of my friends have commented that my current situation seems like a sitcom. Take a lifelong bachelor and workaholic, throw him in a home overnight with a fiancée and her two children, and watch hilarity ensue.

Well, if my life is a sitcom, then ladies and gentleman welcome to sweeps week, the time of year when every television show introduces a major plotline in hopes of garnering that week's highest rating. Or perhaps this is my sitcom's "jump the shark" moment, that moment when a dying television series comes up with a new and crazy plotline, hoping of winning back its lost viewers. Or perhaps this is just life…

Amy and I are having a son … I am having a biological son. **Yeah, you read that right … AMY AND I ARE HAVING A BABY.**

Cut to commercial break so the viewers of my sitcom have a moment to digest that new plotline.

Yes. Life moves pretty fast. A year ago I was single. Come July, I will have three children. Wow! (Yes, July. Amy is almost 18 weeks pregnant.)

On July, I will have a whole new laundry list of issues with which to deal. My list will not include the regular bullet points about which most new father's worry. I am not worried about changing diapers or whether or not I am ready to raise a child or how a child will suddenly affect my life. I have already dealt with and moved past those issues. My list is much more complicated:

- Will I shower my biological child with too much love and make my step-children feel left out? I don't want to and I hope I do not act so selfishly. I would not do something like that on purpose. But, I have never had a piece of myself sitting on my lap before. I have no idea how I will subconsciously act.

- Will I shower my step-children with too much love and not give enough to my own child? This is also possible. I may make such a concerted effort to make them feel loved that I ignore my own child.

The Overnight Family Man

- Will my step-children accept this new baby? They are aware that he is coming and seem happy about having a new sibling, but once their mother's love has to be shared by yet another new face in the home, a face that is not 100 percent related to them, how will they react? They have already had to accept the fact there is a third party in the home – me – whom their mother now loves. How will they react to a fourth?

- Will my step-children accept my biological son as their full sibling or will they treat him like an outsider? Amy's children already have a close bond. Will they feel so threatened by a half-brother that they will lash out at him and never accept him, or will they accept him with the same type of love with which they have accepted me?

- How will my son react when the ex-laws come to town and take Amy's children out on the town for fun and he is not invited?

- How will my son react his brother and sister's father comes back into the picture and takes them out on the town for fun and he is not invited?

- How will my family treat my step-children? It is easy to bond with a blood relative. Bonding with a non-blood relative is tougher. Will my family subconsciously ignore my step-children and shower my son with love?

- Will having a separate blood families in the picture create a rift between the three of them?

- And so on. I could list my fears for another 10 million words if I so inclined.

I can't begin to tell you how excited I am to have a child on the way. I dream every night of what he will look like and be like. All I want to talk about with my friends and family is the upcoming birth of my son.

Yet, I am also scared. There are so many issues with which I will have to deal. Normally, fathers go to their own father for advice. With Amy's children, that is exactly what I have done. Whenever I have a question about being a father, I call my dad. Hell, whenever I have a question about anything in life I call my dad for advice. I have never had to deal with anything in my life without the help of my father. But my father never had to deal with a situation such as this. He cannot dispense advice upon me this time.

Amy and I are alone on this one. There is no one in our lives who knows the proper ways to handle this situation.

Life moves pretty fast. And it is only getting faster. I just hope that when I wake up tomorrow and realize that I am 85 years old that I have no regrets with how I raised my children – biological and non-biological.

I'm scared.

3-4-11
Like Step-Father Like Stepdaughter

One of my biggest concerns about Amy and I having a child was the thought that my son would not take on many, if any, of my emotional characteristics or personality traits because I am outnumbered in the house 3-1 by Amy's family.

Amy's children are Amy. They may not look exactly like her – her son is identical to the father and her daughter is a 50/50 mix of the two – but everything else about them is pure Amy. The way they walk, talk, smile, eat, whine, cry, sigh, laugh, show affection, and so on are all identical to the way Amy does each.

It is easy to understand why. The father has never really been around. They only way they know how to act is from Amy. They are her clones.

I always found this cute and endearing, plus, it made it easier for me to fall in love with her children. It was impossible to fall in love with Amy and not her children because they have 100 percent similar personalities. But, recently, this fact became less endearing and more worrisome.

I think any father wants some of his qualities and personality traits to pass on to his children. I think it is normal to want to look at your child and see yourself in them; not just physically, but personality-wise. I also think that the younger siblings mimic the older ones as much as they mimic the parents. And I know from having a younger brother of my own and from having many friends with younger brothers that this is especially true when it comes to boys; when the younger brother is just a little boy, he goes out of his way to mimic his older brother, which is why so many brothers are alike in every aspect, including the tone and volume of their voices.

Amy and I are having a son, which means he will look at her son as his idol one day. He will purposely mimic everything he does. He will also subconsciously mimic Amy and Amy's daughter. If Amy and her children are all so alike, I thought, I could be outnumbered 3-1. What if my son grows up and does not resemble my personality at all? What if he becomes a third Amy clone? I love Amy more than anything in this world, so that would not be a bad thing. She is perfect in my eyes. BUT, from a pure egotistical standpoint, I want my son to be like me.

Two Tuesdays ago, while playing flag football, my worry was placated.

Amy's daughter has recently adopted a new facial expression, a new nasty looking and ugly facial expression. When she gets especially frustrated, stressed or angry, she curls her nose and upper lip up and gnashes her teeth. Amy cringes whenever she sees it. It really is an ugly and unbecoming facial expression, which is magnified by 1,000 on her daughter because she is such a gorgeous little girl. Amy tries to get her to stop making the face, pestering her by telling her how nasty and mean it makes her look. Amy then always turns to me and says, "Why does she make that terrible face?"

I think you know where I am going with this

At flag football two Tuesdays ago, it was fourth down of a defensive goal line stand. I play middle linebacker on my team and everyone knew the fourth down play was coming my way. The other team's bread and butter play was a hard slant in and they lined their best receiver up on my side. The defensive stand rested in my hands.

At that moment, I realized from where Amy's daughter's ugly expression came. Me. As I waited for the snap, concentrated on the task at hand and allowed my competitive nature to take control of me, my nose and my upper lip curled up and I gnashed my teeth ... an expression I then realized I make whenever I am in the midst of a highly competitive moment or when I am extremely stressed.

Amy's daughter learned the expression from mimicking me. Amy may think it is an ugly expression, but now, whenever I see it, I think it is the most beautiful expression I have ever seen. Amy's daughter is becoming a little bit like me.

My worries about my son not becoming like me now seem silly. I am not outnumbered 3-1. The more time I spend with her children the more like me they will become. They will become a personality hybrid of Amy and me.

True, that tosses a few more pounds of pressure on my shoulders. It means that, while they will never be as close with me as they are with Amy and while they are not my blood children, I will have a profound impact on their lives. But I am up for that challenge. I know I am a good person and I know I have my morals in the right place.

By the way ... on the fourth and goal play ... the play did come my way and.........I knocked the pass down! BOO-YA!

3-11-11
My Little Miracle

A letter to my unborn son:

You are not a mistake.

The first fear your mother and I had upon learning of her pregnancy was that people would assume we got engaged because she was pregnant. After all, our engagement date and your conception date are only a few weeks apart. However, we soon said we don't care what people think. We are happy and we know we love one another, we said. Besides, those who are closest to us know we are in love, we concluded.

However, I recently realized we cannot completely ignore the topic. There is one person the question "Did you only get married because of the baby?" will affect – you. I am sure that one day you will do the math and realize that you were conceived just weeks after we were engaged. And when you do, surely you will wonder, "Am I a mistake?"

Let me put an end to that ridiculousness right now.

I am and always have been in love with your mother and she is and always has been in love with me. I have no idea why, but she is. Whether you were born or not, we would have gotten married and would still be married today. Within a few weeks of our first kiss we were lying in her bed discussing how long we needed to date before we could get engaged. We were always sure that we were meant to be together. The only reason we waited close to six months to get engaged was because we were afraid that if we got engaged too soon our friends and family would disapprove. We wanted to get off on the right foot. Merging two lives into one is difficult enough without having your closest friends and family chirping in your ear that you moved too fast.

We got engaged on October 2, 2010. We moved in together on October 20. You were conceived sometime in early November. (You may gag now at the thought of your mother and me conceiving you.)

I will never lie to you. For instance, I won't be the father who tells you that there isn't a monster under your bed. There actually is. And there is a ghost in your closet as well. So, I will admit that you were not planned. Your mother and I did not sit down and have the "let's have a baby" discussion. We were engaged, but we were also a new couple dealing with the things with which new couples have to deal. We also had to deal with the issues with which any couple has to deal when they move in together. Plus, I had to deal with suddenly raising two children and your mother had to suddenly deal with a man helping her to raise her children. She was used to doing everything on her own. Having a new baby was the last thing we wanted in our lives at the time. We were smart enough to know that the stress of a pregnancy and a newborn could destroy a couple as new as us.

Confused? Are you now thinking, "If you weren't planning for me and if having a baby was the last thing you wanted when I was conceived, how was I not a mistake?" Keep reading.

The fact that your mother and I ever fell in love is amazing. Her friend was my roommate's girlfriend for two years before we ever met. When her friend would offer to set your mother up with my roommate's friends, I was never on the list. We were and still are so different that she never thought we would hit it off. When your mother and her friend went out on the town with my roommate and his friends, I was never invited. I did not enjoy hanging out at the same places my roommate and his girlfriend frequented.

The only reason your mother and I met was because a few days before my team's softball season one of our female players quit. We needed a woman to fill out the roster spot and your mother's friend recommended we call your mother. If your mother had dated one of the guys her friend recommended or if the female player on my softball team had never quit, your mother and I may never have met or dated and you would never have been conceived. We also did not think we could have a baby. I won't get into the medical issues we faced, but we did not think we could have a baby without a medical procedure.

Because we did not think we could have a baby, we did not use protection of any kind. (Feel free to gag again.) When we found out you were conceived, we were shocked to say the least. We were not sure how it was possible. We were sure, however, how difficult it would be to bring a new member into such a new family. We knew that couples who have been together much longer than us struggled with the hurdles a new couple must leap when having a baby. We knew that our unique situation would make it all the more difficult. BUT, we also knew from the moment we learned of your conception that we wanted you. The two A words never entered our minds.

You were not supposed to be possible. But God gave you to us anyway.

My son, you are not a mistake.

You are a miracle.

You are not yet even born and I love you more than I thought possible.

With love,
Your Dad

3-12-11

Facebook Update
I am watching ESPN on the couch with a beer and my 900-year-old dog. Good Saturday night.

3-15-11

Facebook Update
I hope my 6-1 flag football team does not choke tonight in the playoffs. Whenever we kick ass in regular season, we somehow get smoked in the first round of the playoffs. So confusing.

3-15-11
Facebook Update
I am sick to his stomach ... yeah ... we lost... we choked again.

3-18-11
Kicked from the Cool Kids Club
I have a freakishly good long term memory.

I have a nursery school memory of the day my friend Brian had pink eye and had to sit in the teacher's lunchroom by himself while waiting for his parents to pick him up. He cried so hard that the biggest green booger I have ever seen in my life was hanging from his nose like an icicle. When I told him this story recently, he did not believe me that it happened. He had no memory of it. He then told his parents what I said and they confirmed that he did indeed have pinkeye in nursery school. They could not confirm the booger.

I remember the first shot I ever made on the basketball hoop my father built in our backyard. Actually, it was the first shot I ever took on that hoop. My father finished erecting it, climbed off the ladder and tossed me the ball while I was in full stride, running from the swing set. I caught the ball and in one fluid motion tossed it at the hoop. It swished. My father then turned to my sister's best friend's father, Mr. Williams, and yelled, "Woa! Swish!"

I don't just have memories. I have clear memories of almost my entire youth. Amy sometimes marvels at how I can remember specific meals I ate when I was 5-years-old, but how I can't remember to do simple errands I was told to do 100 times. It is just the way my brain works. The tiniest moment in present day life can trigger a memory of something that happened to me over 30 years ago. For instance, seeing a kid crying in a room by himself could trigger a memory such as my friend Brian's pinkeye.

Now that I have two kids, memories are triggered faster than ever before. Everything they do and everything we do together reminds me of a moment from my early childhood.

The memory I am currently stuck on is my father's black Camaro. I don't remember ever driving in it, but I remember the day he sold it. It was right before my brother was born. He sold it for a station wagon! Not any old station wagon mind you, one of those hideous wagons they made in the late 1970s and early 1980s that had the faux wooden panels on the door. Dear lord it was ugly! My dad went from a bad ass black Camaro to a station wagon. It was the day my dad officially got old. It was the day he officially was thrown out of the Cool Kids Club. I was only 4 years old at the time; however, I can still remember the look of defeat on his face when he drove that wagon off the car lot. He tried to act happy about it, but he was such a bad actor that even a little kid knew something was wrong. Of course he did not want that station wagon! What man would rather drive that than a Camaro?! He had to buy it. His third child was on the way and a Camaro was no longer practical.

What triggered this memory? I need to buy a new car, a car capable of handling three children. I don't drive a Camaro. I drive a tiny Hyundai Accent. There is nothing fancy about it, but I've owned that car for six years and am very content driving it. I don't want to drive a different car. Amy keeps reminding me that I have to give it up before the baby is born. I have to get a car that can handle three children.

She wants to get a minivan! Let me repeat that … SHE WANTS TO GET A MINIVAN!

I knew it was only a matter of time before I had to get a new car. Currently, I never take both kids with me at the same time. I usually just take the boy to and from school, drive him to T-Ball and do "manly" things with him such as go to basketball games and take him to the arcade. Amy rarely asks me to take both kids at once. That is a responsibility for which she does not think I am yet ready. However, when the third is born, she has told me, I will have graduated to two-child days, perhaps even three-child days. For that, I will need a bigger car.

Why can't we get an SUV?

She already has the world's biggest SUV in which to transport the kids and it is not as practical as one would think. We live on the outskirts of the city, a place for which it is not meant. Its large doors make parking impossible. Every time we open the doors for the kids there is the fear one of them will push the door into one of the two cars we had to squeeze between.

Doors in general will become an issue when we have to take all three kids anywhere. We will be outnumbered. We will no longer each be able to grab a kid to place in the car. Or, worse yet, on days when one of us has all three, getting three young kids into a giant SUV will be next to impossible. Our hands will be outnumbered! One of our hands will have to grip two children's hands while the other hand carries a baby. Opening doors while making sure that none of the kids wanders into the line of traffic is always a worry; doing it while outnumbered 3-2 or 3-1 becomes nightmarishly difficult.

The solution: One of those fancy mini-vans with the doors that slide open with the touch of a remote control button. We can open the door from afar and herd the kids in. It will make life much easier.

Amy's plan is to use the minivan for trips when all three kids are in tow. We will switch use of vehicles depending upon what each person's day entails. I will have to drive a minivan at times. And, to be honest, her SUV is not that cool either. It has "soccer mom" written all over it.

Amy's plan makes sense. That does not mean I am happy about it.

I am not a car guy, as evident by the fact that I drive a Hyundai Accent. I bought the car for its in-city driving practicality. I am not one of those guys who needs a muscle car to feel like a man. Yet, driving a soccer mom SUV or a minivan scares the crap out of me. I guess it is because it makes me look so old and so geeky. Deep down inside, we all like to believe we will always be looked upon as a cool kid. Even as our 30s begin to inch closer to our 40s, we like to think that 21 year olds look at us as a "cool adult." Driving a soccer mom SUV or a minivan officially kills that vision.

Most fathers get to slowly gravitate towards the minivan moment. They have one kid and realize that their car is not practical for a child, but it is doable. They then have a second kid and still fight to keep their car, like I am sure my father did, but begin to realize they are on the losing side of the battle. When the third comes, they are already mentally prepared for the big change. They have known it was coming long enough to come to grips with it.

I jumped into the shark pool covered in blood.

I went from zero to three kids overnight. There was no slow preparation.

The day is coming ... I will soon be officially old and I will soon have to hand in my Cool Kids Club membership card.

3-31-11
Facebook Update
My home office has been overtaken by two wet dogs on a tornado heavy day. It is so disgusting in here that even I, a dog lover, want to vomit.

4-1-11
Title: Another Letter To My Unborn Son
Dear Benjamin,

Today I wish to explain to you how you were named.

Your mom and I sometimes like to joke that you were actually named after Dora the Explorer's friend Benny the Bull or after a character from your mother's THEN-favorite movie, *How to Lose a Guy In 10 Days*. (I stress the word "then" because I pray that by the time you read this your mother has found a better movie to call her favorite. I also pray she never makes you watch it. The film is so girlie that men are actually compelled to sit down to pee for a week after viewing it.)

The truth is, you are named after one of my best friends. My old college roommate was named Ben and he was like a brother to me. We skipped classes together. We lay in fields together, looked up at the stars and philosophized about life as only college kids can. We sat outside liquor stores and begged people to buy us beer. We ate cold pizza and drank warm beer together. We drank too much together on numerous occasions and both ended up lying on the floor and puking in buckets. We mastered the art of hacky-sacking together. We took long drives, blared Jimmy Hendrix and puffed on "cigarettes" together. We changed from preppie freshman to tie dye wearing seniors together. We were one another's wingmen. We played practical jokes on one another. We talked about love and breakups and our futures. We bitched about classes and how meaningless they felt when we were freshman and discussed how much we enjoyed studying topics we were interested in during our later years in college. We even drove cross country together. We grew from know-it-all college freshmen to know-nothing college graduates together. If you do not yet have such a friend, you one day will and you will then understand what a friend like Ben means.

My friend Ben and I were supposed to grow old, raise families, visit one another once a year and reminisce about all of the good times we had together in college as our children and wives rolled their eyes over having to hear the same stories year after year.

Life does not always turn out the way we want.

When Ben was in his early-30s, he succumbed to the depression that had plagued his life. When Ben was in the prime of his when he had a beautiful wife and young son, he took his own life.

On the day that I write this, it has been nearly three years since his death and I still cry whenever I think of him. When certain songs are played on the radio that remind me of him, I cry. When I flip through the television channels and come across one of his favorite movies, I cry. Whenever I see a group of young kids hacky-sacking, I cry. I miss him so much. It crushes my soul that we did not get to experience a full life together.

He was an amazing man.

Also amazing is the fact that it was your mother's idea to name you after him. She never met him. He died years before we met. Yet, because she knew how much he meant to me, she suggested we honor his memory through you.

That is why you are named Ben.

And, perhaps more importantly, that explains why I love your mother so much.

How you got your names is just the start. There is so much more I want to tell you.

You are going to be born in a few short months.

I cannot wait to meet you.

4-8-11
Who's Your Daddy?

I sometimes worry that my son won't treat me like I am his father.

We had our sonogram last week. On the drive home from the doctor's office, Amy and I jokingly bickered about whom Ben looked like. Amy saw her side of the family. I saw mine. And we once agreed that perhaps he looked like my brother, which started the whole, "Should we get a DNA test?" line of jokes.

When we arrived home, we showed the photos to Amy's 5-year-old son and asked whom he thought Ben looked like. He emphatically replied, "Like my daddy." Huh? He is only 5, after all, and has no idea from where babies come. All he knows is that when his sister was born, his mother's stomach swelled up, a baby appeared a few months later, and he was told that his father was his sister's father. He thinks any baby his mother births is also his father's baby. However innocent his response was, I was still flustered by his answer.

Amy laughed it off and said I was silly that such a statement bothered me. She said Ben would know I was his father. But, Amy's son's statement did not bother me because I think Ben will think that Amy's ex-husband is his father. There are other reasons.

Amy's son has always called me Paul. We tried to come up with a catchy nickname for him to call me but we could never find one that stuck. So he simply calls me Paul. It never bothered me. I don't find the fact that a little boy calls me by my first name to be disrespectful.

Amy's 2-year-old used to call me Pepa. Amy and I guessed that she called me by that name because the only man she knew prior to me was her grandfather, so she probably thought all men were named Pepa.

Amy's daughter mimics everything her brother does, from the way he eats to the way he pronounces certain words. If he decides to get up and run in circles, seconds later she follows his lead and begins to run in circles. She mimics him so well that at times we cannot tell who is calling for us, the boy or the girl. Recently, she began calling me Paul rather than Pepa. It makes sense. She mimics his every move; he calls me Paul thus she will call me Paul.

Ben will surely be influenced by their behavior. He will mimic both of them. He will hear them calling me Paul. Will my own son call me Paul? To most this seems like a silly worry. However, how many of you have ever been in this situation? It seriously worries me that my son will call me Paul. I know that as he gets older he will call me dad. But, when is 2 or 3, he may call me Paul. If he does so outside of our home, I will be humiliated. I know this sounds silly to some, but this is my reality and one that scares me.

4-22-11
Facebook Update
I can't wait for 2030 ... I think that is the year I will be able to take a vacation.

4-22-11
The Big Production
Dear Amy,

I have a confession to make. I lied to you. I never wanted to be your friend.

You often lament how you believe our relationship worked from the start because we were "friends" for two or three months before we ever kissed. Ha! It is hilarious that you believe that I ever looked at a woman as gorgeous as you as a friend. I was trying to get you into bed from the very start. I was not looking for a relationship, however. I wanted you to become a "friend with benefits." But, a funny thing happened on the road to casual sex – I fell for you. Before we ever kissed, I had fallen for you.

About a week or so before our first kiss, I began talking about you with some of my friends. I told them how I'd met an amazing woman and I had never connected with anyone like her before. I told them how we would talk for hours without taking a breath and how when we were not talking we were either texting or emailing. We were 24/7 "friends." I never mentioned you by name of course. I did not want anyone to know that the girl I was pursuing was my roommate's girlfriend's best friend; I would have been humiliated if you shot me down and everyone knew I pined for you.

Plus, everyone would have tried to talk me out of pursuing you; they would have told me I was crazy for pursuing a girl with two kids and an ex-husband like yours.

I was nervous when you invited me over your house on April 23, 2010 to watch a movie. You reiterated time and time again that we were just two friends hanging out, but something in the back of my mind said we would become more. I've dated way too many women in my life so I know the difference between friends, friends who may turn into casual sex friends, and friends who are about to begin dating. The way we'd hit it off, I knew you were the latter. No, you fell into a category I had never broached before. You fell into the "future wife" category. Yes Amy, before we ever kissed, I knew you were the one for me.

We have had our ups and downs because of it. We have yelled and screamed at times and I have slept on the couch a few nights. The arguing has been the toughest adjustment for me. I am 35 years old and you are the first woman with whom I have ever been in love, which means you are the first woman I have ever worried about losing. At times when the pressure of our situation would explode into a fight, my greatest concern was that we were done; that we were not going to be able to make it work. I have had quite a few restless nights, praying that we would be ok. We always have been. I have learned that petty or even major arguments do not cause a permanent rift in two people who really do love one another.

It has been a tough year at times. But it has also been the happiest year of my life. People often ask me if I miss being single, if I miss sleeping in and going to bars whenever I want and watching sports every night and only having to worry about myself. I always tell those people that I honestly do not miss it at all. I would never want to live another day without you and your kids by my side. I love the three of you more than I could ever put into words.

One year ago – April 23, 2010 – will forever be one of the greatest nights of my life. It was the night we kissed. It was the night this crazy journey began.

I love you more today than ever before. You are the mother of my children. You are my soul mate.

This has been the greatest year of my life.

Happy Anniversary.

Paul

P.S. Yes, a love letter to you that thousands of prying eyes get to read. Now THIS is a BIG PRODUCTION!

4-23-11
Facebook Update
I killed the world's biggest spider today.

4-25-11
Facebook Update
I am eating a sandwich packed in a fire truck lunch box. Haha ...Amy even gave me a rice crispy treat.

4-29-11
A Disney Date
A friend recently lamented to me that he has not heard me tell a poopy diaper story in a while.

I hated to break it to him, but poopy diapers are currently not part of my life. It feels good ... and smells better.

Yes, life is perfect for Amy and I right now, the type of life about which they write romantic movies. For instance, Amy and I spent the anniversary of our first kiss on a fairy tale of a date. We both dressed in our finest clothes; she wore a formfitting dress and I wore a tailored suit. We then dined at Bern's Steakhouse, munching on delectable cuisine as we stared longingly into one another's eyes. Next, we took in a romantic movie, snuggling up close and commenting on how addicted we are to one another's smells. Finally, we sipped wine under the beautiful Florida night sky, basking in the peace and quiet of the world around us. It was perfect ... ...

HAHAHAHAHAHAHA!!!!

Ahhh ... and anyone who believed that B.S. is either dumb or single. Nights like that don't exist for couples with two young children and a third on the way. Let me now explain how we really spent our anniversary.

The night began with dinner – turkey sausage and pepper sandwiches that Amy cooked. The sandwiches, as is everything Amy cooks (kiss up time) were delicious. The children were watching cartoons in the kitchen and were sharing a rare moment in which they were not fighting. To disturb peaceful children is like disturbing a sleeping lion that has not eaten in a month. We decided to dine in the den. We could not sit next to one another, though. For some reason, whenever the children spot us sitting next to one another they have to drop whatever they are doing, rush over to us and begin climbing on top of us until one of us gets hurt or they begin physically fighting.

So we had to sit on opposite sides of the room, as far away as we could, and dared not speak. If the children heard us having a pleasant conversation, our few moments of peace would have been ruined. Adults conversing inspires them to empty the toy chest we have in the den all over the floor.

Our evening's plan was to take the children to watch a Disney movie in a nearby park Sponsored by our community's civic association. I dressed in my finest pair of ratty shorts and my nicest T-shirt. Amy dressed in her favorite pair of sweat pants as she frustratingly tried to find a shirt that fit over her pregnant belly. (I will be murdered for writing that last line, I know it, but it is true. One of the toughest parts of Amy's day is trying to find clothes that fit her rapidly expanding incubator of a stomach. Ben is going to be a BIG baby. *Blind Side!*)

It was shaping up to be a romantic anniversary.

The movie turned the romance up another notch. Amy and I had never smelled so exquisite; nothing says romance like the stench of bug spray. Combine that with the scent of the cheap microwave popcorn everyone was munching, citronella candles and someone's kid's poopy diapers, and it was a true gift for anyone's nose.

The movie ... If only I could remember what the movie was. It was hard to pay attention while the child sitting in front of us ran back and forth in front of the movie screen, screaming, "My chair is really big! Does anyone else notice how big my chair is?! It is really big! My mommy gave me a big chair! I'm a little boy but my chair is really big! Does anyone else notice how big my chair is?! It is really big! My mommy gave me a big chair! I'm a little boy but my chair is big!" I wanted to leap to my feet, grab the child's chair and toss it into the Tampa Bay. Seriously, to the family sitting in front of me – your child is a complete tool. There was nothing cute about what he was doing. It was downright obnoxious. Buy your child some loose-fitting underwear because when he hits high school it is wedgie city for him.

Amy's children were actually being perfect angels. They weren't watching the movie; they were digging in dirt. But, they were two of the only children not ruining the movie by running, screaming, fighting or crying. Amy and I took that opportunity to cuddle up and relax.

As I wrote earlier – big mistake! Never get too close to your significant other when the children are being good. A mere second after our hands touched, Amy's daughter dumped a double-handful of dirt on my head ... joy.

The kids behind us then began playing tag. A child a few families away began making fart noises on his arm as his father cheered him on. A mosquito the size of a bear found the one spot on my body not lathered in bug spray – my right foot – and bit off my big toe. And when I again tried to cuddle up next to Amy again, Ben kicked me in the stomach. Yes, you read that right. Even my unborn son won't let us get too close. He sometimes delivers kicks powerful enough that I feel them through Amy's stomach.

We never made it to the end of the movie either. With 30 – 40 minutes left in the film, we decided to call it a night. The children were getting antsy, that scary "We are tired and doing all we can to stay awake" type of antsy. Nothing good happens when children get that tired, unless you consider a mound of dirt being dumped on your head a good thing.

We packed up our things and headed home, but not before Amy's daughter threw an epic tantrum, screaming to everyone in the park that she did not want to leave. Of course, no one in the park could hear her over the half dozen other tantrums being thrown by other kids at that exact moment.

Thankfully, the kids took a quick bath and went right to bed. It was still early. We still had time to celebrate our anniversary.

We contemplated relaxing on the couch and watching a movie.

However, after a few seconds of debating what to watch, exhausted, we decided to instead go to bed ... at 10 p.m. ... on a Saturday night.

By going to bed, I don't mean we celebrated our anniversary by "going to bed." I mean we seriously just wanted to go to bed.

Moments before we both fell asleep, Amy turned to me and said, "Long night."

"Hell yeah," I muttered.

"You still love me, though, right?" she joked.

"Wouldn't change the last year of my life for anything in the world," I said, meaning every word of it.

5-6-11

Facebook Update:

I am gearing up for the arrival of Benjamin Guzzo ... 8 - 12 weeks from now he'll stop torturing Amy's ribs and start torturing all of us.

5-6-11

Mama's Baby

Amy's 2 ½-year-old daughter is not losing her baby status without a fight.

She has been the baby of the family for her entire existence. But, when Benjamin is born, there will be a new baby in the family. The reality of the situation has just recently hit her and she is fighting to keep the "baby" title.

Over the past few weeks, her once rapidly expanding vocabulary has been shortened to one simple phrase, "I'm mama's baby!" She is not asking if she is "mama's baby," she is reminding us in no uncertain terms that she is "mama's baby."

She has been asking for her sippy cup with a bottle-like nipple more than ever before, calling it her "baba," the baby name she used to have for her bottle. She demands that she wears the one-piece pajamas in which she used to sleep when she was a baby. The pajamas are a size too small and look ready to explode when she is squeezed into them, but she is willing to deal with the discomfort to make her point – she is "mama's baby!" She has even begun confiscating any baby toy in the house. She walks around with multiple baby toys in hand, repeating over and over again, "I'm mama's baby!"

Amy and my reaction to this situation has simply been, "Whatever." Of course she is going to be jealous. She is only 2 ½ years old, after all. She doesn't yet possess rational thinking skills. In her mind, she is being replaced. She does not realize that it is possible for her mother to have a new baby and still love her as much as she always has.

Amy said that it could get worse when Ben is born. Perhaps her daughter will demand to drink from a bottle again when she sees the baby with one. Perhaps she will regress to a diaper. Perhaps her vocabulary will continue to regress and she will begin talking like a baby. Whatever … It is not worth butting heads with a 2 ½-year old over something so silly. If she wants to act like a baby again, so be it. If it makes her happy and secure, so be it. It is not like she will be plotting some diabolical plan to assassinate the baby and take his spot. She just wants to act like a baby again.

No matter if or how she regresses, Amy is pretty sure it will be very temporary and that her daughter will surely feel ridiculous about acting like a baby after a few weeks. She said her daughter will realize that she is in fact a "big girl."

Big girl … what an odd phrase to attach to Amy's daughter. I have only known her for one year, yet she has grown so much in that time. When I first met her, she was still in diapers 24/7, she ate with her hands in a baby chair, she was sleeping in a crib and she cried whenever she did not get her way … ok, well, one thing hasn't changed. When I first met her, the only phrase she ever muttered to me was, "My big toe hurts." She often scraped her toe on the steps of Amy's pool and she knew that when she told me her big toe hurt I would shower her with attention. Now, she sometimes sits next to me and mumbles on and on for minutes. About what, I sometimes have no idea, but she is talking full-time nonetheless.

The changes in Amy's daughter have been outstanding and I am proud that I have witnessed a few of her firsts. I missed her first words and first steps; Amy and I had not yet met. But, I did witness the first time she used a toilet. Amy had one of those plastic potty training toilets in her living room. She stripped her daughter's clothes off and, as she did every day, asked her daughter if she wanted to "go pee pee in the potty." And, as her daughter did every day, she stared at the toilet as though it would bite her butt off if she got too close. So I cheered her on … I started chanting, "Pee pee in the potty, pee pee in the potty, pee pee in the potty." Moments later,

Amy's son joined in. We were both enthusiastically chanting, "Pee pee in the potty!" The excitement of the moment got to her and minutes (yes, we chanted that for minutes) later she sat on the toilet and she pee'd! It was exciting! That night I met some friends at the bar and bragged about the moment. They looked at me like I had three heads. What the hell did they care about a little girl peeing in a toilet? Regardless, I was excited.

I was also there the first time she went to ballet. Whenever Amy's son is ready to go to tee-ball, we have a ritual of high fiving and yelling, "Baseball!" Before Amy's daughter left for her first day of ballet, she ran up to me, grabbed my hand, high fived it and yelled, "Ballet!" It was one of the cutest and funniest moments of my life.

Then, this past Monday, we dropped Amy's daughter off for her first day of school. It was hard. We were expecting her to cry and run to Amy and beg her not to leave her. We were expecting her to bang on the window as we walked away and cry for her mother to come back. We were expecting the school to call us that morning, telling us that she has not stopped crying since we left … none of that happened. We dropped her off, she sat down next to another girl and began to play, and we left. No tears. None. She was a big girl about it. For some strange reason, I had a hard time accepting that she didn't cry when we left. When I first met her, she would shed "end of the world" tears whenever her mother left her alone for a few seconds. Now, she was being left for the day and was perfectly fine with it.

When the baby is born, we expect Amy's daughter to have a problem with accepting the fact that she is no longer the baby. What I did not expect is that I am having a hard time accepting the fact that Amy's daughter is no longer a baby. Last year when I met her she WAS a baby. Now, she is growing up.

This is weird.

5-9-11

Facebook Update:
I cannot believe that iCarly and Victorious are going to share the same TV screen!!!

5-13-11
Sugar Daddy

I thought I was getting the hang of this parenting thing. Then, I faced every parent's mortal enemy – sugar.

The Harlem Globetrotters were in town a few months back and Amy and I thought it would be a good experience for her son and I to share. With Benjamin on the way, it is more important than ever for her son and I to bond. We do not want him to think that because Ben is my blood son that he is more important to me. He has to understand that I love them both equally. Getting her son interested in sports seems like the perfect way for us to grow closer – a real father-son experience.

I had two main goals for the game:
1. I did not want him thinking that this was real basketball. I wanted him to understand that this was "theatrical" basketball and that in real basketball it is not legal to pull down your opponents' pants or to throw a bucket of water on the referee. I envisioned him playing his first game of basketball with his friends a few weeks later and running around the court trying to strip everyone naked.

2. I wanted him to at least make it through half the game before he got bored. I have a few friends with baby boys and they all believe that when their sons are 5 years old they will dutifully sit through professional sports games with them and cheer on the favorite team from beginning to end. Anyone who believes that – STOP THINKING IT! Few 5 years old can sit still for hours straight. Sure, there are some who can, but chances are your son will be spastic like the rest of the boys.

The first goal was pretty easy. Five year old boys may be on the verge of frenzied nuclear meltdowns at all times, but they are not idiots. After telling Amy's son once that the game was fake, he was deeply offended that I felt like I had to tell him a second time.

"I know Paul!" he howled. "You told me already! I am not allowed to pull boys' pants down."

That was good enough for me.

The second goal was much more difficult. Amy said the best way to get him to sit still is to give him popcorn. He may not watch the whole game, she said, but he will catch enough in between shoveling handfuls of popcorn into his mouth to make the price of the ticket worthwhile. So that is what I did. Before we took our seats I bought him the biggest tub of popcorn he had ever seen ... and by the end of the first period I had eaten it all. I love popcorn. In retrospect, I should have gotten two tubs. I sometimes forget what a skinny fat kid I am.

"Paul," he said in a shocked tone, "you ate the popcorn all gone!"

I felt like the biggest jerk on the planet. I had to make it up to him, so I bought him the biggest bundle of cotton candy they sold. Oh, what a rookie mistake.

Amy's son handles sugar worse than any human being ever created. Seriously. I have seen him eat one M&M and bounce off walls for over an hour. I once saw him eat one tootsie roll at 6 p.m. and not fall asleep until 2 a.m. I once saw him chew one piece of gum and become so wired he actually cleaned the toy room. I saw him lick a Tootsie Pop once and pull a car from a ditch.

You can imagine what happened to him at a basketball game after he swallowed half a ton of cotton candy. By halftime, when the sugar began coursing through his veins, our seats were useless. He had no desire to sit down.

He began racing up and down the arena stairs. He stood in the aisle and spun around like a top, screaming, "I am getting dizzy!" yet spun for another few minutes. When I finally convinced him to sit back in his seat, he kicked the seats in front of us nonstop. Luckily, my scruffy beard and a freshly shaven head made me look like a complete meathead. The office drone father in front of us turned once to yell, got a glance of my tough guy façade and turned back around. I am not a meathead, however. I am actually kind hearted. Not wanting us to be a nuisance to those watching the game, I grabbed Amy's son and moved us to an empty row in the back of the section.

For the next 10 minutes, he raced back and forth, to the end of the row and back, time and time again, screaming those complete nonsensical noises that only other uber-hyper little boys seem to

The Overnight Family Man

understand. I now understand what inspired the Tasmanian Devil's language – sugared up little boys. Hell, they even spin in circles like the Looney Tunes character when they get too overexcited.

I tried to calm him, but it was useless. I sat there the entire time, my head bowed in defeat, unable to do a thing to stop him.

"You must be a rookie," yelled a voice from the aisle. I turned to see what appeared to be a 500-year-old usher wide-eyed smiling at me. "Must be the first time you've taken him to a game."

"Huh?" I grunted.

"Only a rookie would give a kid sugar this early in a game," he explained. "You give sugar mid-way through the third quarter of a basketball game, beginning of the fourth quarter of a football game and before the seventh inning of a baseball game. You hang it over their head the whole game – tell them they have to be good to get the sugar. By giving it so late, by the time it hits them hard the game is over. They go crazy on the ride home from the sugar high and then crash when they get home."

What a wise man, I thought. Who would have thought that the smartest man I would ever meet showed people to their seats at the Forum. Although, for all I know, he could have been Father Time. The man was old.

"Thanks," I said and then told him what a genius he was, explaining that the boy was my soon-to-be-stepson and I was still learning.

"No problem," he shot back. "I was a rookie once too. I had five boys in all. We all learn in time."

Yep ... I'm learning. Little by little.

5-30-11
Facebook Update

I spent hours cleaning our back screened in porch so that the kids could play in it for two minutes before saying they wanted to go inside ... joy.

6-1-11
Facebook Update

I am skipping work and going to a Rays game today ... very last row in the stadium, just like Amy's son wanted. He doesn't want to sit right on the field again. He thinks the close seats stink compared to the ones really high up.

6-2-11
Facebook Update:
I will not let my son become a writer... UFC champ maybe, but not a writer.

6-3-11
Facebook Update:
I feel like Jessie Spano ... TIME! There is never enough time! I'm so excited ... I'm so excited ... I'm so ... I'm so ... I'm so scared.

6-3-11
I Miss My Family
For the first time in my life I am homesick.

I have not seen my father in eight months. And I have not seen my mother in a year.

They live 1,200 miles away in New Jersey; the only way to see them is by planning a trip. I used to fly to New Jersey for at least one of the major holidays – Thanksgiving, Christmas, Easter or Arbor Day – and again for my nephews' birthday parties. But, I spend all my holidays in Tampa with Amy and her kids now. Plus, Amy's kids are too young to fly unless completely necessary; I detest people who toss their little kids on a plane and make everyone else on the flight miserable as their child squirms or throws tantrum after tantrum. Add in Amy's pregnancy and the cost of flying four people even if the kids were complete angels and us making it to New Jersey this year was not going to happen.

To put into perspective how long it has been since my parents and I have seen one another on a regular basis and how much my life has changed over this time, my father has only met Amy twice and her kids once. My mother has yet to meet Amy or her kids. Amy is my wife-to-be who is carrying my baby. Her children are my mother's grandchildren now. Yet they are total strangers. My parents talk to Amy and her children on the phone as often as they can, but there is a disconnect because of the lack of face-to-face time. However, I know this is only a temporary problem. I know my parents will soon be visiting Tampa on a regular basis.

My mother had been dealing with severe heart palpitations over the past six months and my father did not want her to travel until she received the necessary surgery to remedy the problem. She is now healthy and ready to come meet my new family. I know that once the baby is born, my parents will be in Tampa often ... but what about my sister?

My sister Nicole also has two children – a 2- and a 5-year-old and she is not ready to fly with them. How long will it be until I see her family again?

It eats me up to know that I am a stranger to my nephews. I have met her oldest on a handful of occasions, but he is just now at the age in which he is recording lifelong memories and I am not part of any of them. I have not seen my youngest nephew since his first birthday party; as far as he is concerned, I do not exist.

However, what really bothers me is that Amy's children and our soon-to-be son may never develop a strong relationship with their cousins. This is a thought that was brought on by this past Memorial Day, a holiday I always looked forward to because it meant I would be hanging out with my Cousin Michele.

My cousin Michele has always been more than a cousin to me. She is a second sister. We saw her for every major holiday – Thanksgiving Christmas, Easter, Fourth of July, Labor Day, Memorial Day, Veterans Day, President's Day, Earth Day, and so on. We had a close knit family. If there was a holiday that allowed us to have a sit down dinner or barbeque, we got together. I also saw her for anniversaries, graduations, weddings, funerals, birthdays, my sister's ballet recitals, her ice skating competitions, spelling bees, etc. Throw in the fact that she stayed with us for a month every summer and it is safe to say I rarely went more than a few weeks total without seeing her.

I have so many fond childhood memories of my cousin. She is the reason I am a Mets fan. She is also a big reason I am a Dallas Cowboys fan. She is actually the person who taught me how to throw a football. And every summer, along with my brother and sister, we spent hours upon hours at the local pool.

My sister, I am sure, has even fonder memories of Michele. They shared a room when she stayed with us. They attended the same college. They are more than friends; they are best friends.

Amy and my kids won't have that type of relationship with their cousins on my side of the family. It may be a few more years until they even meet. In time I know they will. Much to my chagrin as a Mets fan, my sister's kids are Phillies fans. But, that does mean that when they are old enough they will probably make annual treks to Tampa Bay for Spring Training.

I also know that Amy and I will one day want to make annual trips to New Jersey. However, seeing your cousins once or twice a year is not enough to form a true relationship. They will know one another as cousins, but will they ever be friends?

I was also very close with my mother's sisters and my father's brother. Visits from them were always exciting. My brother lives in Tampa and I know he will grow close with my family. But Amy and the kids will barely know their Aunt Nicole. They will barely know anyone in my family.

I miss my family. What makes me so sad is that my son and Amy's children may never miss them. You cannot miss those you do not know.

6-10-11
Dropping Some Knowledge

What is the coolest thing about becoming an overnight family man? I skipped ahead to the fun father-son stuff! I didn't have to suffer through spit up on my shirts, poopy diapers or the terrible twos before I could enjoy hanging with a 5-year-old boy.

For example, in the past few months I have:

- Introduced Amy's son to *Ghostbusters* parts one and two and they are already his two favorite movies in the whole wide world! There is nothing quite like passing on one of my favorite movies to the younger generation, even if it means I have to watch the worst movie ever made – part two – from time to time.

- Taken Amy's son to TWO Rays games. He had been to at least one Rays game already, but it was years ago so his games with me will be his first memories of baseball. The first game was courtesy of my father. He bought us tickets just five rows from the dugout. It was the closest I have ever sat to any sporting event and I was blown away by the view. Amy's son, however, was unimpressed. He wanted to sit, "Way up high!" So for our second game we bought nosebleed seats and sat in the very last row. He loved it and has bugged me on a daily basis to take him again. I hope he always loves those nose-bleeds. I'd rather pay $7 than $70 any day. I know I am not that lucky, though, so will enjoy it while I can.

- Watched the new *X-Men* movie with Amy's son. This was our first "no girls allowed" movie date and I was worried that he would not be able to make it through the entire film – it is 132 minutes and keeping a 5-year-old's attention that long is harder than … well … nothing is harder than that. But, I want him to be a comic book movie and super hero fan. So I decided to give it a try. The movie did not start off well. The opening scene was in German with subtitles. He cannot read yet. He squirmed around and began making fire truck noises for no reason whatsoever. It looked bad. However, once the X-Man took center stage, his eyes lit in amazement as they showed off their super powers. As soon as the movie was over he begged me to take him to see the *Green Lantern*. I'm so excited. I have a new movie date!

- Taught Amy's son to throw a football. Our efforts to teach him to play tee ball have not been successful. And when I say unsuccessful, I mean unsuccessful on the same level as the last *Indiana Jones* movie. He has the ability to be a good player, but he is not yet interested in the game. Although, if playing in the dirt ever becomes a scoring play in baseball he is bound for the Hall of Fame. However, I showed him how to throw a football a few weeks back and he picked it up immediately, zipping perfect spirals to me time and time again and had a blast doing so. If I can get his mother to stop cringing when she pictures him playing competitive football, we may have a future Cowboys quarterback on our hands.

- Bought his first NERF basketball hoop for his bedroom. Now I know why my parents hated my NERF hoop. The constant sound of him running around his room, jumping off his bed and crashing to the floor as he tries to slam dunk the ball has caused me to develop an eye tick. But, it is exciting to know that he loves playing my favorite sport – basketball.

These are the types of things men dream about doing with their sons and I got to do them all during my first year of fatherhood.

But, there is also a downside to becoming a father of two

before I was ever a father of one. It is more difficult to enjoy those moments most first-time biological fathers get to experience.

For instance, the first time we heard our baby's heartbeat was a terribly stressful experience for me. While Amy was marveling at how fast it was beating, I was busy breaking up a fight between her two kids. It was nothing major; normal brother-sister fighting – a little pinching, a little pushing and a little WWE-style chair shots to the head.

Amy asked if I heard the heartbeat and I said I did, but I actually did not. All I heard was the voice in my head counting backwards from 10, trying not to explode in frustration.

Then there was the first ultrasound. We only had one child with us that day; her son was in school. But it was just as stressful. As I wrote a few weeks back, Amy's daughter is jealous of the new baby. Whenever we cooed over the ultrasound pictures of the developing baby, she pinched my leg to draw my attention back to her. After a few pinches and after losing a pint of blood, I decided to give her all my attention. It was much easier that way.

With that all in mind, Amy and I have been worried about what we are going to do with the children when she goes into labor. Her sister lives 40 minutes away, works fulltime and has a newborn of her own.

My brother lives nearby, but he works fulltime so he may be in a meeting when we try to call. And he goes out at night, so he may not hear his phone ring if the bar is loud. Plus, he is single. I am not sure he is up to the chore of looking after two kids

Her parents are deceased and mine live 1,200 miles away. My parents would fly down to help us, but they both have fulltime careers and there is no way to know when Amy will give birth. The only way they could be sure to be here for the birth is if they took a month off work, which is not possible.

We have a sitter, but we cannot be sure she will be available when Amy goes into labor at night unless we book her for an entire month.

As the birth of my son grows closer, I am beginning to worry that I may have to miss his birth. I may have to look after the other children.

Then again ... afterbirth, screaming and a baby with the

weight of a bowling ball squeezing out of Amy ... maybe that is a good thing.

Yes, being an overnight family man has its benefits!

6-16-11
Facebook Update:
Amy and I are thinking that Ben will be born in 3 - 5 weeks, despite what the doctors say. God, if my son is half the stubborn jerk that I am, your kids are all in trouble.

6-17-11
Apparently, I Smell
I've known pregnant Amy longer than I have known non-pregnant Amy.

I think I remember that non-pregnant Amy was tolerant, rational and level headed ... I think ... because the only Amy I know now is pregnant Amy, who is ... well ... anything but rational!

Excuse me as a duck a right cross ... Amy is reading this over my shoulder as I type it. Relax, I'm joking ... I would never write this entry around Amy. I'm at my office. I use work as an excuse to get away from the crazy woman!

On a serious note, if I no one hears from me next week please send police to my house and tell them to follow the smell to find my murdered corpse.

Speaking of smells

I think I remember that non-pregnant Amy enjoyed cuddling up close to me and kissing me as I slept. I think I remember non-pregnant Amy loving to embrace me randomly throughout the day and telling me how she can't get enough of me. I think ... because the only Amy I know now is pregnant Amy whose sense of smell is so powerful because of the hormones raging throughout her body that there are times she gags from my scent. "You smell like the outdoors," she has said to me on numerous occasions. She has also regularly told me such things as, "You smell like the dogs," "You smell like the gym," and my all time favorite, "You smell like a urinal cake in a bus station bathroom." Topping the smell insults is the look on her face. She looks utterly disgusted, as though she could vomit at any time. Yes, nothing boosts your confidence like the woman you love being on the brink of vomiting because of your scent. Luckily, I have a few of friends with pregnant wives and they have all been told similar things, allowing us to realize that we do not smell; the women are crazy!

I think I remember that the non-pregnant Amy used to love to sit outside with me and talk the night away as she sipped a glass of wine ... I think ... because the only Amy I now know cannot drink wine and only has nasty things to say to me as I drink beer after beer and rub it in how good they taste and how I would never be able to go so many months without the sweet, soothing taste and affect of alcohol. Yes Amy, beer and wine taste even better than you remember. In fact, scientists say that alcohol has never tasted better than it has over the past eight months but unfortunately the epic taste is going to fade in July. Oh, wait, is that when the baby is born and you can drink again? Wow ... sucks to be you.

If my car does not leave the driveway for a few days, tell my parents I loved them.

I think I remember that non-pregnant Amy used to love to dress up in sexy dresses and confidently sashay around town with me, turning heads everywhere we went as men and women alike murmured, "What the hell is she doing with that guy?" Actually ... that is one thing that has not changed. Amy is still gorgeous. Seriously, she is stunning. She complains as she searches through her wardrobe for something to wear that she feels gross and unattractive and hates going out in public looking so pregnant, which proves how crazy she is. While she says she has never felt less attractive, I have never been more attracted to her!

Amy often laughs that I got royally screwed because I fell in love with "skinny and sane Amy" and ended up spending over half of our time together with a different woman. She is partially right. She is a different woman. The hormonal imbalance and physical discomforts that come with pregnancy have definitely made her edgy. There are times that I walk on eggshells around her. But, I do not feel as though I got screwed because she is no longer "skinny and sane Amy." As odd as it sounds, the reason I am more attracted to her than ever before is because of how miserable she has been. Yes, she is one of the most gorgeous pregnant women you will ever see; she still turns heads when we go to the pool or the beach.

However, it is mostly the hell she is going through that is drawing me to her rather than her beauty.

She is carrying my son. We will both get to revel in the joys he will bring us, but only one of us has to physically suffer for 9 – 10 months.

I will be forever grateful to her for going through this ordeal yet again. She already had two children, but she loves me so much that she wanted to have at least one more so that I could have a biological child of my own.

If you don't hear from me soon, don't bother me. Amy would never hurt me. She loves me too much. If you don't hear from me, I have not been kidnapped or murdered. Rather, I am voluntarily rubbing Amy's sore back. She deserves it.

6-23-11
Facebook Update:
I will just be staring at Amy's belly for the next week and waiting for the sign ... lowest my eyes have wandered while looking at pregnant Amy in months.

6-24-11
Father's Day Firsts
About two weeks ago I realized that this year would be Amy's son's first Father's Day memory. He is 5 years old but has not seen his biological father for almost three years. He was too young at 2 years old to know what was going on. He has never had the opportunity to knowingly wake up to a father figure on Father's Day.

Her son was jumping with excitement for two weeks. They had already purchased my present and he was bursting to give it to me. At least once a day for two weeks he would whisper to his mom, "How many more morrows until we give Paul his surprise?" [Two notes about her son: 1.) His "whispering" is louder than most kids' yelling. 2.) He calls days "morrows" because he thinks "tomorrow" means two days.]

A few days before Father's Day, I walked into the kitchen and Amy's son was busy with the crayons. When I asked him what he was drawing, he said, "A card, but not a card for you." A minute later he asked me how to spell Paul and Father's Day. Amy's son will definitely never be a spy or a ninja.

The night before Father's Day he continually asked Amy if she was going to make me breakfast in the morning, reminding her that it was, "Paul's day." And when he saw her baking a cake that read, "Happy Father's Day Paul," his excitement grew to a whole new level. I honestly think he was more excited on Father's Day Eve than he was on Christmas Eve. The cake also amped up Amy's daughter. She began running around the house, clapping her hands together and yelling, "Tomorrow is cupcake day" and "Tomorrow is Paul's Mother's Day!"

Amy's son woke us up early the next morning, jumping on the bed and yelling that he has a present for me. It was a beautiful coffee mug that she made with the kids. Her son painted the entire mug blue, which he suggested because he remembered me telling him that it was my favorite color. Amy then wrote both her kids' names on the mug as well as Ben's name, and the word "Dad" on the handle. Needless to say, I loved it.

Amy's son asked me 100 times if I liked it and all 100 times that I said yes he jumped up and down squealing in delight. He then bestowed another handful of gifts upon me – pictures he drew of me and him holding hands with a fire truck behind us.

It was a perfect morning. The perfect first Father's Day as a father.

Of course, the greatest present I received was one that did not come in a box or drawn on a homemade card. The greatest gift was that my first Father's Day memory as a father is also Amy's son first Father's Day memory as a son. How cool is that?

Then, as Amy and I prepared for sleep that night, she bent over in pain for an instant. Ben is kicking she said; kicking her cervix. He is not supposed to come for another six weeks but she can feel that he wants out well before then. Ben is coming. He is coming VERY soon. Life is about to change yet again.

6-29-11
Facebook Update:
I have Ray's tickets on the third baseline today at noon ...

yeah ... Ben is definitely coming today.

7-3-11
Facebook Update

My dog's anxiety is getting out of hand. She has not sat still all day. She has just been pacing back and forth, barking and crying. I have tried valium, Benadryl, melatonin and even tried to mix all three ... nothing works anymore. She is 18 and just going crazy.

7-4-11
Facebook Update:

Amy was hoping for a Fourth of July birthday for Ben ... 90 more minutes to make it happen. If not, I want a 7/11 birthday. Not only is it the homerun derby this year, but I can begin a tradition of buying him a Slurpee every birthday!

7-7-11
Facebook Update:

I think it is obvious that Ben will be as stubborn as me ... he was ready to come out and then the doctor said he would be born within 13 days ... he immediately stopped trying to get out. Seriously, Amy's contractions and the head butting of the cervix stopped the day the doctor gave us that news. It's like he heard it and said, "F U! I'm staying put now just because you want me out." Yep ... that's my boy.

7-15-11
The Fate of the Guzzo Name

If my son is ugly, is it my fault?

If he is stupid, is it a knock on my genetics?

There are already certain genetic flaws he could inherit that will be easy to pin on either Amy or me.

I already know that if he grows up to be bald, he inherited that gene, or lack of a hair gene, from me.

If he only grows hair on one side of his legs, that's my bad as well. It's one of my most embarrassing traits.

If he has a lisp, then it is probably from my genetics; I had a lisp when I was a kid.

And if his bones are brittle, that is definitely from my side of the family; my brother and I seem to get hurt on a weekly basis.

If Ben is a sweaty kid, that's all her.

If he needs to drink five gallons of juice an hour, that's definitely a result of her bloodline.

(Amy is not a sweaty woman and she would kill me if I allowed the readers to believe that she is. But her kids ... wow! I used to wonder why her kids needed to drink so much. Then, I saw them running around outside. Within five minutes they both looked like they had just finished running a marathon in the desert.)

Amy's son, however, is freakishly smart. He can build some of the most amazing things I have ever seen a little kid erect. For instance, after we drove over the bridge on the way to the Rays game, he came home and built an exact replica of the bridge using Tinker Toys, Legos and blocks, mimicking the bridge's arches, railings and even the cameras on the poles; it was amazing. He also recently built an elevator out of Tinker Toys that can actually go up and down.

If Ben can dance, that's Amy's doing. Her daughter, at just slightly under 3 years old, has the type of rhythm most white adults would kill for. (Actually, perhaps dancing should be put on the list of bad characteristics Ben could inherit. I do not want a son who can dance. Nothing, and I mean NOTHING, is more obnoxious than a white guy who can dance. He can be the nicest and most down to Earth man on the planet, but if he dances in public he is automatically blacklisted by 99 percent of the other white men in the room.)

And, both her kids are adorably cute.

With Amy having two kids boasting so many of the traits parents want their kids to have, what if Ben does not exhibit these same characteristics? What if he is stupid?! What if he looks like a troll?! What if he turns out to be a Communist?! Amy will always have the leg up on me in arguments when we debate whose fault such characteristics are! "The other kids are fine," I can imagine her saying, "so he must be dumb because of you."

I already hear it from my sister. Her 5-year-old son is a freak athlete, the child who instills fear in the hearts of the kids on the other team because he kicks the soccer ball or hits the baseball too hard. My sister laughs that he obviously inherited his athleticism from her husband since no one in our family was ever that good of an athlete. My sister gives her husband's bloodline all the credit!

If Ben turns out to be a dud, perhaps the Guzzo bloodline is tainted. Perhaps that will be the sign that my brother and I should get snipped before we corrupt the population with more of our kind.

Ben ... you better be the smartest and most handsome baby of all time! I expect you to find a cure for cancer, break Barry Bonds' career homerun record, date Carmen Electra and paint a perfect replica of the Mona Lisa ... all before the age of 2! The honor of the Guzzo genetics rests squarely upon your shoulders!

It's a lot of pressure, but if you can't handle the heat then get the hell out of the kitchen my boy!

To anyone reading this who took any of my insane rants seriously: You may want to begin checking into your own bloodline to figure out from what side of the family you inherited your gullibility and stupidity.

7-18-11
Facebook Update:
I am a biological father.

7-19-11
Facebook Update
Now that I am a biological father, I plan on hourly posting about how cute my kid is, how smart he is, how nice he is, and so on ... I will place him in a different online contest each day and expect you all to vote for him ... and every cute photo I post I expect hundreds of people to comment, "Awww." And I expect you to pretend that he is not an alien, despite his head looking like Sam Cassell's.

7-22-11
Welcome Benjamin Guzzo To The World
"Paul, my water just broke."

Amy said the words calmly, as though she was telling me the time of day or what we were having for dinner, and she said it quietly enough as to not wake her kids in the next room. Yet, somehow, the sentence crept into my ears and woke me from a deep slumber at 4 a.m. on July 18, 2011.

"Huh?!" I said as I sprang from my bed.

"Baby Ben will be here in a few hours. We have to hurry," she whispered, rather stoically for a woman who must have been in pain. This was her third time giving birth, though, so it was old hat for her. The great thing about having a baby with Amy is that I have never had to experience the first time dad fears. Amy is an expert so I just trust her instinct on everything.

"Call your brother right away," she ordered like a manager dolling out assignments to his workforce and remaining calm as she grabbed her stomach in pain. "Tell him we'll be at the hospital soon."

Amy's sister could not watch the kids because her baby came down with Roseola a few days earlier; perfect timing. We had to rely on my brother. He had never babysat children in his life and we needed him to watch Amy's kids for only God and Ben knew how long.

Plus, my brother had informed me the day before that he was suffering through a multi-day migraine. I placed a call to him and told him we were desperate. Tired and still in agony with the migraine, he readily agreed to help. I am forever in his debt. If not for him, I would have missed the birth of my child because children are not allowed in the delivery room.

It took us over an hour to get out of the house. Amy showered. We packed breakfast, lunch and snacks in a lunchbox for the kids. I threw Amy's overnight bag in the car while Amy packed toys and a change of clothes into a backpack for the kids. I then placed the pajama-clad kids in the car while Amy made their beds. Yes, you read that right; she took the time to make all the beds.

My brother was not yet at the hospital so I had to stay in the waiting room with Amy's kids until he arrived. Amy was in pain and alone. It was killing me not to be with her.

When my brother showed up I left him with the kids and rushed to Amy's room. Unfortunately, it was the wrong room; security gave me the wrong room number! I busted into the room and stumbled upon a strange half naked woman lying in bed, screaming in pain and breaking her husband's hand with her grip. I apologized, wished them luck and sprinted back to the security guard to get the right room number.

I finally found the right room and was thankful I walked into the wrong one first. Amy was also screaming in pain and I knew better than to let her hold my hand. Hey, I'm a writer people! I need my hands!

Her contractions were one minute apart for two hours before the anesthesiologist finally arrived to administer her epidural. During the wait, we held our breath every time footsteps approached, hoping it was the anesthesiologist, and were disappointed over 100 times. Yes, I counted. I had to do something to pass the time. I couldn't talk to Amy. She warned me the day before that when she gave birth that she wanted me in the room but did not want me to talk to her unless spoken to. "I will be in extreme pain," she explained. "And if you try to talk to me I could take my pain out on you and say something I will regret. I love you too much to want to be mean to you."

When the anesthesiologist finally rolled his cart into the room, he was called out moments later to help with an emergency C-section; her epidural would have to wait until he returned! I have never seen anyone look more deflated than Amy was at that moment. She went from the brink of bliss to not knowing how much longer she would have to suffer. It was a terrible tease.

In the meantime, to help with her pain, the nurses gave her a shot of a morphine substitute that promptly got her higher than Cheech and Chong on a bender. Just a few minutes later, the anesthesiologist returned and administered the epidural … OH MY GOD! IT WAS HUGE! It was terrible to watch, but she seemed to enjoy it as her pain immediately subsided. Then, she realized that she was stoned out of her mind from the morphine – "I can't remember how to breathe," she exclaimed in total fear like a college sorority girl smoking a joint for the first time. I wanted to laugh at how high she was; I have never even seen her drunk, let alone Bob Marleyed out of her mind. But, her next words sucked any humor out of the situation, "I may be too high to hold the baby. I didn't even need that damn pain killer. The epidural guy came right back." It was heartbreaking. I had been praying for weeks for Ben to hurry up and be born. At that moment, I was praying that he would take a little longer, just long enough for Amy to sober up.

The midwife checked on Amy and told her the affects of the morphine would wear off before the baby came because she was nowhere near giving birth. With time to kill, I decided to run my brother and the kids back to my house rather than forcing them to be cooped up in a hospital all day. Back at my house, I gave my brother and his girlfriend, who arrived to provide him help, instructions on how to care for the kids. I threw a whirlwind of instructions his way – where the kids' cups were and which were their favorites; the proper way to prepare their juice; what they can and cannot eat; where their favorite toys are and who has the rights to which coloring books; how to bribe them if they act up; who he should call if there is an emergency and cannot get a hold of me; and so on. As I rattled off countless instructions, my brother stared wide eyed and mouth agape, a look on his face that said, "Who the hell are you and what have you done with my brother? This is a real father standing in front of me!"

As I raced back to the hospital, I called Amy to tell her I was on my way and she cried into the phone, "Hurry up please. Something went wrong." HOLY SHIT! I have never driven faster in my life or thrown more curse words at random drivers in my way.

In my absence Amy had a bad reaction to the drug the nurse gave her pre-epidural. Her blood pressure dropped so low that the room filled with doctors who were worried that she could die from an overdose. She was stable by the time I arrived, but still shaking in fear.

The next few hours were thankfully uneventful. Amy spent the time trying to shake the morphine cobwebs from her brain and I sat quietly waiting ... waiting ... waiting for the midwife to check on Amy and tell her the baby was coming. Oh yeah, I was shivering. No one told me that delivery rooms are colder than meat lockers and all I was wearing was shorts, a T-shirt and sandals.

Then, shortly after 2:30 p.m., when my lips could not get any bluer, the midwife announced Ben was ready to enter the world. A few pushes and out he came; the midwife even allowed me to assist with the delivery. Amy freaked! She began yelling, "Paul drops everything! He is the clumsiest guy I know! Don't let him drop the baby!"

The midwife placed my hands on Ben's body as he was

squeezed from Amy's body. My first memory of meeting Ben is that he looked mad ... REAL MAD! As though he was thinking, "What the hell?! Why did you kick me out of my home?!"

He was born at 2:49 p.m. on July 18, 2011, weight 6 pounds, 12 ounces and was 20 inches long. He was the tiniest person I have ever seen in my life.

The midwife then let me cut the cord, which was disgusting, like cutting through a piece of raw chicken. I was offered the opportunity to carry Ben to the baby bath tub a few feet away, but I turned it down so I could wash the two gallons of blood off my arms! It was awful! It turned out I made the right decision. As a nurse carried Ben to the bath, he fired a stream of pee right at her face and hit her in the mouth. That's my boy!

As I watched his first bath, I noticed he had the largest testicles I have ever seen in my life! What a boy! When I exclaimed it out loud, the nurses laughed and said that was normal; they were just swollen and would return to normal. I am saddened to write that they were correct.

Amy and I then held Ben for an hour and marveled at how cute he was. Ok ... actually, I laughed at how funny looking he was. His nose was swollen from the delivery and his head looked like an alien's. I said he looked like Sam Cassell, a former NBA player whose odd-shaped head earned him the nickname "Alien."

I am happy to say that both his nose and head now look normal ... well ... kind of.

He looks just like me. Poor kid. Hopefully, he got his mother's hair. Two Guzzo men should not have to suffer with this face and no hair. And with me raising him, we know his personality will suck.

By the way, have I mentioned that I have a SON?!?!?!?! WOW!

7-29-11
Facebook Update:
We took Ben out for his first night on the town last night ... a late night at Channelside at Wet Willies ... I had a stiff drink and he was a bobble head ... felt like I was hanging out with one of my friends circa 2004 again.

8-5-11

Twenty-Five Percent

Twenty-five percent. That was the chance that our baby would be born with a deadly disease.

Five months ago, Amy and I found out that we are both carriers of the cystic fibrosis (CF) gene. When two parents carry the gene, the baby has a 25 percent chance of inheriting the gene from both parents. If a baby is born with two cystic fibrosis genes, he or she is born with the disease.

Amy was never tested with her other two children because it is only recently a required test. Neither of her children have CF and none of her close to 100 living cousins has it or has been diagnosed as a carrier, so there was no reason to believe Amy is a carrier. I was never tested because I have never had a reason to be tested. One of the ramifications of an unplanned pregnancy is that neither party has pre-pregnancy testing to make sure they will not fall into the "at-risk" pregnancy category.

Normally, if someone told me there was a 25 percent chance that something could go wrong for me, I would look at it as meaning there is a 75 percent chance that nothing will go wrong. But when those odds had to do with my unborn son, 25 felt more like 25 million. Never before had the number 25 seemed so high in value and so ominous.

We did not learn that we were both carriers until month four of the pregnancy. It was too late for an abortion, although neither of would have wanted one anyway. And it was also too late for the fetus to be tested for CF; at the four-month mark the fetal test could result in brain damage. So we had to wait … and wait … and wait for five excruciating months to find out if our baby would be healthy or not.

The question, "Would I be destined to outlive my son and watch as he slowly died rather than lived his life?" haunted me day and night. There was no range of emotions during these five months of mental anguish that included acceptance. Anger, fear and pity, but no acceptance.

Anger towards my family …my mother had a cousin who died of CF and my sister knew she was a carrier. My family knew there was a good chance I was a carrier, yet they never told me.

When I broke the good news that Amy was pregnant, they never thought to mention that we could be birthing a child with a deadly disease so perhaps we should get tested!

Twenty five percent ...

Anger towards God ... I sat up many nights cursing God for daring to hurt my son! "WHO DO YOU THINK YOU ARE?!" I would demand. Or, I would break down in tears and yell to the heavens, "Whatever it is that I did wrong, do not punish my son! IT IS NOT FAIR! DO NOT PUNISH MY SON!"

Twenty five percent ...

Anger for everyone who tried to comfort me. Friends and family kept telling me, "There are children who suffer from worse diseases" and "I know a kid with CF who has lived a fulfilling life." All I wanted to reply was, "SHUT UP! I don't care what other kids are suffering from! I don't care if other kids with CF are happy! I don't care about other kids! The only kids I care about are my own! I just want mine to be happy! If it sounds selfish, deal with it! Stop trying to make me feel better! You cannot! My son may already be dying!"

Twenty five percent ...

Fear ... fear that I would not have the courage to deal with watching my son die from the moment he was born.

Twenty five percent ...

I also feared what effect it would have on Amy's children. It is hard enough for young children to deal with a new baby stealing some of their attention. It is another situation all together for young children to have to cope with a new baby who needs constant medical attention. A CF child would have a major impact on their lives; Amy and I would never be able to be there for them as much as other parents because we would have to constantly make the CF child's health our primary concern; they would always be second fiddle.

Twenty five percent ...

Pity ... self pity ... My job as a father is supposed to be to protect my son, not give him a deadly disease. I placed all the blame on my shoulders. It was my fault. If I was not a carrier, he would have no chance of being born with CF.

Some nights, the self-pity was overwhelming. I would kiss

Amy good night and tell her I would be in bed in an hour after a television show I wanted to watch was over. Then, I would sit in the living room alone and cry uncontrollably for my unborn son. Dear lord I shed a lot of tears.

When he was born and I finally held him and put a face to the love I felt for him, the self-pity was even more unbearable. I could not fully enjoy his birth. I kept looking at him wondering if I had murdered him or not. He was so ... he was so amazing ... he was my son ... and all I could think was that he was sick and it was my fault!

Twenty five percent ...

The night after he was born, I wept like I have never wept before. I wept until my head was in the toilet.

Twenty five percent ...

For one week, as we waited for the results of his blood work, everything he did was a sign that he had CF. If he pooped too much, CF. If he did not poop enough, CF. If he had the hiccups, CF. If he coughed, CF. I swear the worst thing to ever happen to parents is Google!

Twenty five percent ...

Then, the day of the results finally came. He does not have CF. He is not even a carrier of the gene! He is healthy AND will never have to go through the same anguish I dealt with when he has children.

A few months ago I wrote a, "A Letter To My Unborn Son," in which I explained to him that he was not a mistake; he was a miracle. Today, as I write this, I believe that more than ever. If Amy and I had gotten pre-pregnancy tests and learned we were both CF gene carriers, we may never have tried to have a baby.

There are again tears in my eyes as I type. But this time they are tears of joy.

8-12-11

Facebook Update:

I am so proud of my son ... word came back from London today ... he is being knighted ... from this day forward, Ben Guzzo will also be known as Sir Poopsalot.

8-12-11
Not The Mama!
My son is confused ... real confused.

Because both of Amy's children call me Paul, I am always worried that he will grow up thinking he should call me Paul. He is my son; of course I want him to call me dad.

However, before he can call me dad, he first needs to realize that I am not his mother!

I know what many of you are thinking and you are correct. I am beautiful for a man and I do smell like a goddess at times. But, there is nothing womanly about my figure ... or so I thought.

Whenever I hold Ben and place his head against my chest he ... well ... he thinks it is mealtime. And when he doesn't find what he is looking for, he doesn't give up easily. He begins pulling his head away from my chest and slamming it face first, mouth wide open, back into my chest time and time again, like a hungry bird. And after he does this for 30 seconds to a minute, he gets angry, real angry, Incredible Hulk angry! His face turns beet red, his nostrils flare, his eyes squint and he lets out a howl that could easily be mistaken for a male goat being castrated without any anesthesia. It is a frightening sound! He then continues to head butt my chest while screaming until Amy rushes into the room and grabs him from me. Here is the real kicker – sometimes when she grabs him and tries to feed him ... he is not even hungry!

Other times, she hands him to me immediately after she feeds him so I can burp him, and he still tries to feed off me! He may not even be interested in me for my food; he may just want to know what I taste like! My poor son is one confused kid!

I have heard from some of my friends that their newborns did the same thing. One friend said his son actually latched onto his nose one night thinking it was a nipple. It is good to know that I am not alone. It is still a bit awkward ... and it is definitely something I plan on making fun of him about for the rest of his life ... starting ... right now!

8-18-11
Facebook Update:
Amy's coffeehouse, The Buzz, is officially open for

business! Did I forget to mention that she was opening a coffeehouse? Sorry ... I have a lot on my plate. But yeah, all the caffeine we can drink now. Boo Ya!

8-19-11
Facebook Update:
I haven't exercised all week ... just a miserable feeling.

8-19-11
The Obligatory "Newborn Poopy Diaper" Story

With Amy flooded with work due to the opening of her coffee shop, The Buzz, I have become a stay-at-home dad for the next few weeks until Amy has the employees on their feet. The nature of my work allows me to work from home.

However, I quickly learned that stay-at-home parents with newborns have NO free time to work and it is mostly due to food going in one end and out the other.

The first day I was left with Ben for the day, Amy instructed me that he needed to eat every two hours. What she failed to mention was that it took almost two hours to feed him. Ben is the slowest eater I have ever known outside of my Uncle Cliff, a man who would still be on his salad when the rest of the table was enjoying after-dessert coffee.

Ben does not like the formula we give him. He prefers breast milk BUT, obviously, I cannot give him the good stuff he craves. When I run out of the supply left for me, I have to give him formula. It takes five minutes just to get the bottle in his mouth. He twitches his head in every direction. He even tries to push the bottle away from himself. I keep fighting him and pushing it toward his lips and I eventually win; I think he finally realizes the only way he is going to get rid of the hunger pains is to accept that he has to eat the yucky food his dad feeds him.

Once I have the bottle in his mouth, he sucks furiously for 10 straight minutes. His face showcases an expression of concentration and desire usually saved for marathon runners at the end of the race. The boy is working hard! When he stops to catch his breath, I burp him for a few minutes and then I look to see how much he has drank; it is always only around a quarter of an ounce. He has to drink two ounces per feeding! So I go through the entire ritual again!

To compound matters, he poops while he eats. Amy did not tell me about that either. The first day I am alone with him, right after I heard the gurgling noises echoing from his pants (a baby's pooping noise is equivalent to when you used to pass gas in the tub, by the way) I rushed him into my bedroom, where we keep all his changing supplies. For those wandering, yes, he does pee on me from time to time. I can keep him covered up until the last possible moment and the second I expose him the stream shoots into my chest or face. He even got me in the mouth once as Amy's son watched and clapped with joy. Amy's son has since told everyone we see, from friends to complete strangers, about how his little brother peed in my mouth.

On my first day alone with Ben, I wiped and scrubbed his butt, put a new diaper on him, walked back to the living room, where I can get most comfortable on a couch while feeding him, continued the struggle to get him to eat and while burping him he pooped again. So I went back to the bedroom, wiped him, scrubbed him, put on a new diaper, walked back to the living room, continued the struggle to feed him and while burping him he pooped again! He did this one more time! Four poops in one feeding! It took me 90 minutes to feed him two ounces of formula. He then fell asleep for 30 minutes and woke up screaming for more food! AHHH!!! Four more diapers later and 90 minutes I was ready to lay newspaper and a bowl of milk on the floor for him and tell him to take care of himself. If he could crawl yet, I may have! (It's a joke people … relax … the newspaper and milk part, not the struggle to feed and change him.)

I later learned that while I cannot cut the struggle time down, I do not have to waste time changing him during the feeding. Amy and multiple other parents told me to just let him keep pooping during the feeding and even to wait a few minutes after he is done before I change him. Apparently, newborns sometimes digest food instantly; in one end and out the other.

One particular day last week, Ben laid a real stinker during his feeding. He must have pooped a good five times. The smell was overwhelming. As soon as he was done eating, I rushed him into the bedroom to change him. On the way, he was kind enough to throw up half his bottle all over me. I immediately realized why he hates the formula – it smells like dog food! (So perhaps putting it in a bowl would not have been so wrong, huh?)

I laid him gently on a changing cloth on my bed and ripped off his diaper. WOA! There was a sea of poop in there! For those who have never changed a newborn's diaper, their poop is liquid. Instantaneously, Amy's son and daughter came rushing into the room, each crying that the other one was pinching them. As they were yelling this, they were both pinching one another IN THE FACE! And neither would let go! I wish I could say that I had never seen anything like it, but I see the two of them do that exact move at least once a week.

I stunk terribly from the puke, the poop smelled awful, and I had a WWE-style cage fight occurring a few feet from me that I had to break up ASAP. Then, as I rushed to change the diaper, Ben immediately peed everywhere, dousing my shirt. Startled, my hand slipped and splashed into the sea of poop. This was not the first poop finger I have ever experienced. But, that does not change the fact that my immediate reaction was, "OH MY GOD! " I don't know if I will ever get used to poop finger.

I was covered in puke, pee and poop and had two children screaming in pain who refused to stop pinching the other's face ... it was a mess ... and this is my life now.

Wow.

8-20-11
Facebook Update
Working again... so tired. — at The Buzz.

8-25-11
Facebook Update
I work in a coffeehouse but am dead tired ... ironic ... my boss is a real slave driver.

8-26-11
A BUZZ-Y Day
Friday, August 19

The Overnight Family Man

Wake up at 6 a.m.

Amy showers, grabs the baby and hurries off to her coffeehouse so she can open by 7 a.m.

The moment she is out the door I shower, chug a pot of coffee and use the next 90 minutes to get some work done on one of my writing projects before the older kids wake.

The other two kids wake up around 8:30 and need to be bathed because we got home from work too late the prior evening to do so. I scrub them both clean and then fight them over what they are going to wear that day. The son wants to wear his favorite pair of green shorts that are way too small for him and the daughter wants to wear her Hello Kitty outfit that she outgrew months ago. They both win and wear the tight clothing.

Then comes breakfast. First they want cereal, but then they won't eat it because they decided they want a bagel instead. So I make them each a bagel, which they allow to sit on their plates for the next hour as I wash the dishes and clean up the house. They want cereal again, not the bagel, but it has been an hour since the cereal was served and it is terribly soggy and the milk is bordering on rotten, so I have to get them new cereal, which they again allow to get soggy and rotten because they are too focused on the television to eat. SO, I pour them a third bowl and turn off the television, telling them that they cannot watch another second until they eat. They both respond with cries that would make you think I just told them that the world ran out of ice cream. They still don't eat the cereal and instead eat the bagel.

I have to get them to The Buzz by noon because I have a 12:30 appointment to get to, an appointment for which I am unprepared because I have not had time to do the necessary work. I beg the children to go play in the toy room for 30 minutes so I can do some work. Five minutes later they both emerge from the toy room looking like they went 100 rounds with Mike Tyson, as they are both bruised and bitten.

I somehow scan the documents necessary for the meeting while the two kids use my legs as the focal point of their favorite game, Bridge. This game's rules entail them both crawling across my legs as they rest on the living room coffee table. My knees crack under their dual weight at times, but at least I can get some reading done.

    I rush them to The Buzz, where Amy looks like I feel. It has been a busy morning and she has had a crying baby strapped to her in carrier the whole time as she prepared countless lattes and cappuccinos and did her best to ignore the screaming baby as she introduced herself to all the new customers. The look in her eyes as I drop off the other two kids with her is one of defeat. She needs a break, not two more children, but there is no way I could take any of the kids to my meeting. So, she trusts her new business with an employee she has only known for a few days and rushes the kids out of the confines of the small coffeehouse before they kill each other or her business; three kids should not be locked up in there all day.

    After my meeting I rush back to The Buzz to learn that Amy has not yet returned. It was a slow early afternoon, so the new employee was able to handle it, but as soon as I show up a rush of customers arrives and I am forced behind the bar to help make lattes. My hands shake each time I hand a new customer his or her first drink at The Buzz, knowing that there is only one chance to make a first impression and that a bad cup could scare a new customer away forever. To my relief, everyone loves their drinks.

    Amy returns with the kids and is in a state of frenzy when we tell her that there was an afternoon rush without her around. We tell her that everything went OK and we handled it well, but nothing can calm her nerves. There is no time to fret. We have to rush over to her son's school for open house and to meet his new teacher.

    We are the last parents to arrive. The teachers have already left the classroom for the day and have to be called back just to meet us. We apologize and explain that we have three kids and two careers. I am not sure if the teachers care. I don't have time to assess their reaction because the baby is hungry and needs his diaper changed. As I feed him a bottle, I actually try to explain to him that I cannot change him for another five minutes so he needs to chill. This may surprise you, but he does not seem to understand me. Apparently, four-week olds cannot yet comprehend English.

    We hurry back to the shop to relieve the morning employee and then get a call from the afternoon/evening employee that his car has broken down and he needs a ride. I have to pick him up and leave Amy alone with three kids and a coffeehouse to run; my tail

The Overnight Family Man

lights are out, so Amy feels unsafe with the kids in my car. I plan on fixing the tail lights as soon as I have five minutes free ... should be some time in 2020.

Once I return to the shop, Amy and I prepare The Buzz for the evening crowd. While the night employee cleans behind the bar, we clean the bathrooms and the floors. We then rush the kids home for baths and dinner. Amy prepares the dinner as I again bathe the kids. Once dinner for the kids is cooked, Amy rushes back to the coffeehouse with the baby and I stay with two kids who have been cooped up all day. Suffice to say, they are not calm. I believe cabin fever and stir crazy are the apropos terms to describe their demeanor.

By the time the babysitter arrives to relieve me, I am midway through a nervous breakdown. I wish that was a joke, but it is not. As Homer Simpson would say, "No sleep makes Paul go something something."

I head back to The Buzz where we are pleasantly surprised by the evening rush. A lot of beers are drank ... a lot of wine is uncorked ... a lot of laughter is heard ... a lot of new friends are made ... and Amy and I are not involved in any of the good times because all either of us wants to do is go home and sleep. Impossible. Amy is the face of the establishment and needs to be there on its first Friday night and many of the guests are there on my invite; it would be rude to invite people and then leave.

The Buzz closes at 1 a.m.

Amy goes home to get some sleep while I clean the place with the night employee. We finish around 1:30 a.m.

I give him a ride home and then finally get back to my house at 2 a.m.

I slip into bed without a shower, as not to wake Amy.
Saturday, August 20 ...
The alarm clock rings at 6a.m.
Luckily, we have all the coffee we can drink.

9-1-11
Facebook Update:
My son is actually getting kinda cute ... I'm a bit upset. I

enjoyed having the big nosed alien-headed kid. Now his nose is normal size and his head is round. Oh well... at least I can still laugh at him for not being able to walk, talk, crawl or roll over and for not having eyebrows or teeth.

9-2-11
Back To School

Keeping a 2- and 5-year-old cooped up in a coffeehouse all day was not a good idea, but it was the only option we had for The Buzz's first week in business. The kids were hell with legs. They ran in circles around the place. They pinched and hit one another. Add in the baby's constant crying for food or diaper changing, and The Buzz was overrun with our children's wining and crying. They were not being bad; they were just acting like most kids would act who are bored and confined to a small space for days on end. Customers with children understood, but when customers without children came in, their faces told us that they did not understand and we risked losing them forever. I'd like to say I thought, "Screw them! If they can't handle kids we don't want their business!" But that would be ignorant. We are a small business and every customer counts in the opening weeks. Anxiety was overcoming me. Something needed to be done!

And something was done ... school started. The 2-year-old started VPK and the 5-year-old started kindergarten.

The morning I dropped the 5-year-old off at school was one of the few peace-inducing moments I'd had in months. When I hugged him goodbye and closed the door to his classroom behind me, I was filled with relief. Part of me choked up of course; he is growing up, in "big kid school now." But a larger part of me thought, "We can get some work done!"

And we did.

Because of the kids, The Buzz was opened, but it was not complete. We had numerous stores to hit to pick up much needed supplies; dragging three kids into these stores is too much to handle. We also had not had time to market the place. Our business was based on word of mouth and foot traffic. Again, three kids in the place made it tough to focus our minds on such a simple task as telling people we were open.

The moment both kids were in school, Amy and I became a whirlwind of activity. We picked up food and coffee supplies. We made signs and menus. We bought a television and sound system for The Buzz and hooked them up. We contacted networking groups, artists and not-for-profits and set up events. We began a social media campaign to advertise our opening. We completed twice as much in six hours as we did in the entire previous week. With only one child, the baby, we were capable of so much.

When 1:45 p.m. rolled around and I had to pick up the 5-year-old, I was a bit upset. My day was about to get hectic ... and I was ashamed that that thought ran through my head. I love him, yet I felt that the best part of my day was dropping him off at school. I felt like a total jerk. I felt like the worst parent in the world.

The line of traffic in front of the school was 20 minutes long and the closest parking spot I could find was five blocks away, which felt like 50 blocks under the hot Florida August sun. Compounding the heat issues was that I sprinted to the school; it was 2:20 p.m. by the time I parked, five minutes after school let out, and I pictured a distraught 5-year-old boy desperately searching for me after his first day of school.

When I arrived at the school's pick up area, no kids were out there at all. No kids had exited the building despite parents being told to be there at 2:15 p.m. So I sat outside in the heat, waiting and pouring sweat, wondering if the other parents had already labeled me "the sweaty guy."

I was frustrated. I decided that picking him up at school was a curse and I was mad that I was stuck with the job.

The kids finally exited the building at 2:20 p.m. They are told to stay in line and to not run off to their parents until they reach their class's official pick up spot. Then, before they leave, they have to either high five their teacher, hug her or shake her hand so that she knows the student is leaving. Almost every kid in kindergarten broke the rule on their first day, running to their parents as soon as they saw them. The teachers scrambled about, trying to get the children back in line so they could account for each of them.

In the back of the chaotic scene, I spotted Amy's 5-year-old son, one of the few children listening to the teacher, dutifully standing in line as he was told. When he spotted me, he smiled ear-to-ear. He wanted to run to me, I could tell, but he did what he was told.

And then, he hugged his teacher, was told he could leave, ran to me as fast as he could and gave me the strongest hug he had every given me. I was filled with joy and almost broke down in tears; not because he was so happy to see me, but because I realized how happy I was to see him. Those six hours had been the longest I had gone without seeing him in months. He has become my shadow and a man without a shadow is a lonely man indeed.

As I carried him in my arms to the car and smothered his forehead with kisses, he giggled and told me all about his first day of "big boy school" and how much he loved it.

When we reached the car and I strapped him into his car seat, he asked me, "Can you pick me up from school every day?"

"Of course I will," I promised. "It is the best part of my day."

That was not a lie. It really is.

I'm not saying I want him and his sister back in The Buzz from morning to night again. That will never be an ideal situation. Dropping him off from school each day still brings me a sigh of relief, as I know we can get work done.

Kids can be a handful and can be frustrating. No matter how much you love them, you have a breaking point. But, that does not mean you do not love them.

Now, when it is time to pick the 5-year-old up, I am ready to call an end to my work day. I want to spend time with my favorite 5-year-old boy on the planet. I want that hug he greets me with every day.

9-5-11
Facebook Update:
I have been staring at a wall since 9 a.m. ... seriously ... if I put Ben down for one second it is end of the world ... can't work, can't go outside ... can just sit on couch while Ben sleeps on my chest. WHAT A FUN DAY!

9-9-11
I Don't Have a Dream
I am tired of people telling me that I am living every guy's

fantasy by owning a bar in Florida.

I have never dreamt of owning a bar.

When I was in college, my friends and I would sit around at night, sipping beers and talking about our futures, and most of the guys always had the same dream. "I want to own a bar in the tropics," they would say. I always kept my mouth shut during that portion of the conversation. My dream was to be a writer, but I had no desire to chime in with such a dorky notion.

I think most men see owning a bar as the "cool guy job." They envision themselves sitting at the bar all night, sipping expensive alcohol and hitting on all the women who happily reciprocate the advances because they want to be seen with the owner of the bar. Owning one in the tropics is like adding chocolate fudge to ice cream – the women are in bikini-shape all year long!

I never even had the "I want to be a bartender" dream. Most guys bartend for the same reason they want to own a bar – to bed the shallow women who want to be able to brag to their friends that they can skip the line to get in to the popular bar and then get cheap drinks from their bartender boyfriend. The only time getting a job as a bartender crossed my mind was when I thought it would be a great way to meet interesting people to write about. Yes, I am that cool.

So it is a bit ironic that all these years later, I am the only one of my college friends who now has a stake in a bar – The Buzz, which is a coffeehouse by day and bar by night. In truth, it is all Amy's. She dreamt it up, she designed it, she went through the permitting hell, she did battle with the contractors, she chose the coffee brand, she hired the employees and she chose the specific beers and wines and flavors of ice cream to sell. She did it all and The Buzz stands as a testament to her hard work and desire. She dreamt of opening an establishment that would become a true community hangout spot – a place for coffee in the morning, lunch in the afternoon and drinks at night; a place where neighborhood parents could take their children during the day (The Buzz has a toy area and cartoons playing so parents can relax as the kids play), and a place that offers live entertainment so the locals have something to do close to home. The Buzz is her dream come true. I am only considered an owner because … well … because I sleep with the true owner. Our lives are merged together as one; what she owns I own, and vice versa. Unfortunately for her, I don't own much. This is a real one-sided relationship in that regard.

I am involved in the day-to-day operations of The Buzz, however.

I help out as an employee on certain days and watch the kids on other days so she can devote all her time to the business. I am trying to bring events to The Buzz and push for my friends and their friends to make The Buzz their regular spot for coffee in the morning, lunch during the day and beer and wine in the evening. I support The Buzz when she needs me and then work on my career when there is free time. Luckily, my career as a freelance writer offers me flexible hours.

And Amy is just as supportive of my career. When her day at The Buzz is complete and it is my turn to work on one of my writing jobs, she takes on the responsibility of watching all three kids. She is completely worn down and exhausted on most evenings, as she works from 7 a.m. to at least 7 p.m., but she somehow finds the energy to handle three screaming kids alone so I can work.

Most people start businesses either before they have children or once their children are old enough to take care of themselves. We have three young children to raise and two businesses to run – The Buzz and my freelance career.

Such a work schedule is tough on both of us. Though we are around one another almost all day, we rarely spend time together as a couple. We are usually coworkers or parents. Any alone time we can get is coveted. So, when I am done with my work, Amy is free, the kids are in bed and The Buzz does not need our attention, the last place I want to be is at The Buzz. That is where the dream of owning a bar ends and the reality sets in. I was never naïve enough, even as a know-it-all teenager, to think that owning a bar was no work and all play. I never imagined owning a bar as an all day and all night party. I never envisioned myself sitting at the bar all night playing the role of the cool owner. It is a career, like anything else.

Last Saturday night, I swung by The Buzz for a few moments to help the night bartender with a few quick things. A handful of my friends and their girlfriends and a few single women were there. I took care of my small chores and then began to head for the door, but they all called me back. "Dude, you own a bar, sit down and have a drink!" they exclaimed. The single women's ears perked up when they heard that I was the owner. There I was, a bar owner in a tropical climate, all the free alcohol I could drink and a bar full of friends and girls who wanted me to stick around so they could shower me with attention. It was every guy's fantasy come true ... but mine.

All I wanted to do was go home and see Amy. And that is what I did.

9-16-11

A Letter to My Black Hearted Baby
Dear Ben,

The jig is up. I'm on to you. I know you are trying to ruin my shirts.

Ever since I met your mother, she has complained about my wardrobe. She has told me that it is too outdated. She has told me that I look foolish wearing shirts that I purchased in the 1990s. And I have always wholeheartedly disagreed with her. I think the shirts look great on me. Besides, if the 1990s style ever comes back, I'll be the coolest looking father in town.

Her complaints remind me of my childhood. As far as I know, my father only owned one pair of shorts and one pair of jeans, both of which he purchased sometime in the early 1970s. Every day of my childhood, I heard my mother yelling at my father that it was time to buy new clothes; the short-shorts style went out years ago and that bell-bottom jeans were no longer cool either. My father defended himself using the same argument I now use, that one day those clothes will be back in style and he will be the coolest father on the block. He was half right. While the John Stockton look never caught back on, bell bottoms did in the early 1990s. Overnight, my father went from geek to chic! And I think that being looking upon as cool by the fashion gods inspired him because he finally tossed away the booty-choker shorts and bought a modern pair that actually hung to his knees.

But Ben, I know your mother has no desire to wait 15 years for my clothes to be back in style. She wants them gone now and I know she recruited you to rid my closet of them forever!

At first I was fooled. Every time I held you, you threw up on me, sometimes four or five times in a day. I thought that you had acid reflux and it was just a disgusting coincidence that you threw up on me and not your mother. Then your mom made excuses such as, "You jerk him around too much," or "You need to burp him better," and I believed it! I now know that she only fed me those lies because she feared I was catching on and she wanted to buy you some more time. And I fell for her plan, hook, line and sinker.

Perhaps I would have been a sucker forever ... perhaps ... if you had not pushed the envelope a bit too far. Yeah, you know what I'm talking about. You began stretching my neck holes! You know that one of my biggest pet peeves is the neck holes on my tee shirts. I like them snug around my neck. The second one gets stretched I want to toss it in the trash. I hate drooping neck holes! You know this about me! I complain about it constantly when your brother and sister grab my neck holes when we play. There is no way you have not heard my gripes! Yet, every time I pick you up ... EVERY DAMN TIME ... you grab my neck hole and pull on it!

Oh, I know what you are going to say in your defense and it will not work on me! "But daddy, I am just two months old! How I could be part of such a diabolical plan? How could I be intelligent enough to be in cahoots with my mom? And why would I turn Benedict Arnold on my own father?!" Well Baby Ben, if that IS your real name, that reply only gives you away! If you are smart enough to use the words diabolical and cahoots and if you know who Benedict Arnold is, then you are smart enough to team up with your mom to destroy my wardrobe!

True, perhaps you picked up those words by watching Baby Einstein's and perhaps you know about Benedict Arnold because you recently sat on my lap while I watched the Brady Bunch episode in which Bobby has to play Benedict Arnold in a school play. But, even if those were the TRUE reasons, you gave yourself away the other day. You proved that you have quite a bit of Baby Stewie in you.

You know what I am referring to! You were gassy the other day, so gassy that your screams of pain gave me goose bumps and brought tears to my eyes as I thought, "My poor baby is so sick!" Yeah, I believed your act. I was stupid. So I did what I always do when your belly hurts. I put you on your back and pumped your legs to try to push the gas out of your belly and I kissed your feet to make you smile. And you made me believe that it was working! You began to smile that "Oh, aren't I so cute" smile of yours, so I continued to kiss your feet time and again. Then, as I went to kiss them for perhaps the twelfth time, you pulled your feet close to your belly to lure me into your trap, and I fell for it! I followed your feet and when my face got just inches from your butt, you farted. And when I gagged from the smell, I saw you smile! I saw it! You laughed at me!

That is when I realized the depth of your wickedness. Later that night, as I carried a laundry basket full of baby vomit covered tee-shirts with stretched neck holes, I realized that if a baby is black hearted enough to fart in his father's face on purpose, then he would definitely ruin my shirts on purpose!

Ben, you are one evil baby!

Well Ben, give your mom a message for me! You two will not win! I will not get rid of my shirts! I will not buy new clothes!

I am going to see a psychiatrist to help me get over my stretched neck hole phobia. And I will wash each shirt multiple times if that is what it takes to get the smell of baby puke out of them. If the wash does not work, if they still smell, who cares? It will be your mom's cross to bear. Hell, it will be your cross to bear as well! It is one thing to be the smelly man with stretched neck holes. Sure, people will think I am pathetic. But, it is more pathetic to be the woman who is attracted to such a man! And you Ben … of you … your friends will laugh at you because you have the smelly dad with stretched neck holes!

So, no matter what you do, you cannot win!

Love,

Your father

9-30-11
Who Am I?

I sometimes worry that I am going to lose my identity.

Most people who know who I am (and that is not many) know me as one-half of the Guzzo Brothers, Tampa's award-winning independent filmmakers. And that is who I like to be known as. I enjoy my other writing jobs, but nothing fulfills me creatively as much as making movies. While many people know me as a writer, I like to think of myself as an artist. Columns, history articles and biographies are fun, exciting and, most importantly, pay the bills. Making movies, though, fuels my soul. Never was the fact that I love being an artist more self evident than Thursday, September 23, 2011.

My brother and I are working on a new film, called *Who Is Delsin?* It is about a war reporter who is kidnapped by angry Iraqis during the Gulf War, tortured and held for ransom. When the reporter is rescued, the U.S. government claims they did so, but the reporter claims he was rescued by a real life super hero, a "Man of Steel" who deflected bullets and carried him to safety. Determined to prove he is not crazy, the reporter goes on a decade-long search for the man who rescued him, to prove that perhaps super heroes really do exist.

In order to complete the film, we need over 20 pieces of original art. When making an independent film, budgets are sometimes tight, as in "we only have enough money to feed ourselves today" tight. We did not have the necessary capital to pay for over 20 pieces of original art. It turned out, we did not need cash.

On September 23, an art show was held in South Tampa dedicated to our film. Over 20 artists created original works of art inspired by our film and put them on display in a one-night art show. We then photographed the artwork for use in our film. The artists helped us because they believe in our film and they believe in our body of work. To see so many paintings inspired by a story created in my mind was awesome. It was the most humbling experience of my life. I had never felt more respected as an artist as I did on that evening.

While lying in bed later that night, a dark reality clouded my happiness – I have not completed one creative writing piece since I finished the *Who Is Delsin?* script. I completed that script a few weeks before I moved in with Amy and the kids.

There just is not enough time for creative writing anymore. There are kids to support. There are larger bills to pay. There is a new business for which to care.

To do my part in handling all these fiscal responsibilities, I have to take on more paying writing jobs than ever before. Every paying writing job I take is amazing and I am lucky to be able to make a comfortable living solely by stringing words together into sentences. I know writers who would love to be where I am at career-wise. But, the more paying jobs I take, the less time I have to dedicate to creative writing, writing for which I do not get paid until the project is complete and sells ... sells for a very small profit.

Once my work day is done, the kids are in bed and household chores are complete, it is usually around 10 p.m. By that time, my brain is fried and I cannot think of one creative thought.

I am not lamenting that my family holds me back and the doldrums of family life has cramped my creative style. That could not be farther from the truth. I have never felt more fulfilled as a person than I do today. Only a fool would give up what I have for a little boy's dream of earning a living solely as a creative writer. However, there will obviously always be a small part of me that yearns for the artistic fulfillment that the recognition as a creative writer brings to me.

Amy tries her hardest to be supportive of my artistic side. One of the reasons she wanted to start her own business was because she hopes that it will one day make enough money to support the entire family so that I can dedicate my career to creative writing.

However, small businesses are such a crap shoot. We can do everything right, work harder than anyone else on the planet, and still fail. Or perhaps it becomes successful but by the time it does I am yesterday's news and no longer have the necessary credibility in the arts community to complete my creative projects. If I drop off the creative map for a few years, will I still be able to pull off an art show dedicated to my film?

Life keeps getting in the way of life. Responsibilities change. Priorities change. We change. The man or woman you were when you were single and without kids is not the man or woman you are with a family. It is impossible to hold on to every aspect of the single you. Certain parts of the single you are lost in the shuffle of family life. What makes my situation unique is that I was not eased into it. It has all been so sudden that at times it is hard to handle.

I did not get into this blind. I knew when I wanted to marry Amy that it meant giving up the great amount of time I once dedicated to my creative side. I love her enough that I deemed it worth it and it has been. It still does not make it easier to accept. I'm human after all, and part of me wants to have my cake and eat it too.

I have so many stories locked inside my brain that I want to bring alive. But I wonder if I ever will.

I am sure there is a way to be "Guzzo Brothers" Paul and "Family" Paul. I just haven't figured how yet. I hope I do before I lose the "Guzzo Brothers" part of my identity.

I love my family and will give up the "Guzzo Brother" Paul if that is what it takes to raise the kids and help make a small business a success. But if that happens, I know there will always be a small part of me that will wonder "What if? ... What if I did not have to worry about paying the bills?"

10-4-11
Facebook Update:

I love that Walgreens keeps the condoms in the baby aisle. To increase condom sales, I suggest taping my dinner table and playing it on a TV in that aisle.

10-10-11
Facebook Update

I am starting to realize that my son is useless. He can't sing. He can't dance. He can't get a job. He can't walk, talk or even crawl. He doesn't have teeth. He doesn't even have freaking eyebrows yet! What the heck is wrong with this kid?! Get it together!

10-14-11
Facebook Update:

I want Ben to be Mr. Miyagi for Halloween and Amy is not agreeing with it. Someday, when Ben's favorite movie is the original Karate Kid and he finds out his mom ruined his first Halloween by not allowing him to be Mr. Miyagi, he may never speak to his mom again.

10-21-11
The Name Dilemma

What's in a name? In a non-Rockwellian household like mine, everything!

Amy's 5-year-old has been my "buddy," "little man," and

"big guy" since Amy and I moved in together. They are basic and generic terms of endearment/pet names for adults to call kids.

Most fathers call their sons by those names and I stress "sons," as in fathers with multiple sons. These fathers have no problem doubling up and using the same pet name for various sons and the sons don't seem to mind. My household is different, however.

When Ben was born, he immediately inherited these nicknames as well. I would yell to him from across the room, "How you doing little man?" or, "I'll change your diaper in a minute buddy," or "When are you going to learn to walk or at least grow eye brows big guy?" Because, you know, my baby is a genius and can understand what I say. On that note, so can my dog, my mango tree and all my appliances when I yell to them, "Why aren't you working?!"

Talking to my baby did not seem like a bid deal until the day Amy's son responded to one of my rhetorical questions to Ben. I asked Ben, "Hey buddy, what do you want for dinner? Formula, formula or formula?"

"What?" asked Amy's son.

"Oh, I was talking to your baby brother," I replied.

"Then why did you ask me?"

"I didn't," I responded, a bit confused. Did I say the 5-year-old's name? I wondered.

"You said buddy," he casually stated.

I didn't really think too much of it and for the next few days continued to call Ben all the pet names father's use for their sons. Then, a week or so after the formula conversation incident, Amy's son called me on it again. I don't remember what I said to Ben, but Amy's son poutingly said, "Ben stole my names. I thought I was your buddy."

Ouch. That hurt. I felt like a total jerk.

And my nickname errors did not end there.

I also often refer to Ben as "Baby Ben." It has a nice ring to it.

Amy's daughter has adjusted pretty well to the new baby. She had always been "Mama's Baby," so we were a little worried that a new baby in the house taking her spot would cause jealousy that would manifest itself in regression such as not being potty trained anymore. Or, we thought she would lash out by being more disobedient to get attention (I stress MORE ... wow is she a handful!). Neither has occurred. BUT, while she is fine with a new baby in the house, she still wants to be referred to as THE baby. So whenever I called Ben "Baby Ben" when she was in the room, she would flinch and very nonchalantly say, "I'm the baby."

Two kids and two name infringement cases. Something needed to be done.

Some parents may think I am overreacting. (If you are single and think I am overreacting, I don't care. Until you have children of your own, you are not allowed to have an opinion on raising kids.) I am sure some parents are thinking, "Well, of course there will be a little jealousy of the new baby. That is normal in every family but you cannot allow it to consume you."

What these parents have to remember is that I do not have the average family. I am only the biological father of one of my three children. I don't look at Ben any differently than I do Amy's children. I honestly love all three of them the same and I even consider her two children to be MY children, not their biological father's. I 100 percent think of them as my own and I think they look at me as their full fledged father. The 3-year-old girl calls me "daddy" 90 percent of the time and the 5-year-old boy introduces me to his friends as his dad.

However, I fear that as they get older, they will wonder if I love Ben, my biological son, more than them. I wonder if this will cause a rift in our family. So I feel I have to be extra-careful to constantly remind them in subtle ways that I love them just as much as I love Ben.

This is why I have to be careful with this "pet name" issue. I cannot allow them to ever think I gave their names of endearment to Ben.

SO, I no longer call Ben, "Buddy," Little Man," or "Big Guy." He is now just simply, "My dude." It seems to be working. The 5-year-old has not been jealous of his new baby brother since. Plus, Ben seems to love the name. He giggles with absolute glee when I walk into a room and yell out, "My dude!" And, I love it too! I get a total kick out of my son becoming "My little dude."

As for the 3-year-old and the "baby" issue ... I now call Ben "Dude," her "baby" and instead of calling her Ben's "big sister," I tell her that she is Ben's "big baby sister." It sounds so stupid, I know, but it keeps her happy, which is all that matters.

I have been a "family man" for one year. Throughout this year, I have learned that the hardest thing about being a parent is not bathing or feeding the children. It is not getting them to bed on time or breaking up sibling fights. It is not disciplining the children, helping them with their homework or teaching them how to play sports. The hardest thing about being a parent is remembering to do the small things that tell your kids that you love them and that they are each special.

Children love presents, but toys and clothes are only temporary. Affection lasts forever.

10-28-11
The Nap

"What do you want for your birthday?"

It was a question tossed at me for weeks leading up to the celebration of my 36th birthday on October 20, 2011. My parents wanted to know. Amy wanted to know. Even the kids wanted to know. The question was beginning to annoy me. Not because I was not grateful that the ones I love wanted to give me something special, but because the only thing I needed was something that I thought no one could give to me – a nap.

Three kids, a business and a writing career have ripped the word "rest" from my vocabulary. "Single Paul" enjoyed eight hours of sleep a night. Today, four or five hours of sleep feels like a present to "Family Paul." So, a mid-afternoon nap would be the greatest present of all time, I told Amy, my parents, the kids, our dogs, my mango tree and our household appliances.

Ahhh ... naps. I have been a napper my entire life. My mom often laments that I was the easiest of her three children because I was such a great napper. She said that wherever she left me as a little kid, I would fall asleep. I would fall asleep on unfinished basement floors. I would fall asleep in cars. I would fall asleep under desks. I even fell asleep in a bowl of pudding once.

My love of naps did not dissipate with age. In high school, I would often blow off my friends by telling them I had chores to do at home. But I would actually curl up on a couch to reset my mental batteries.

In college, I would set my class schedule around my nap schedule. I always made sure I had a window of time in the early afternoon that allowed me to stop at my apartment for a nap. If I couldn't get back to my apartment, I would sometimes nap at the library. I would even date girls only because they had comfortable beds and apartments or dorm rooms near my classroom buildings.

My napping continued into my adult years. I would sit back in my chair during my lunch breaks and take a 15-minute snoozer. I would later take a second nap around 7 p.m.

But now ... now ... the real world has taken naps away from me. And I HATE it! I miss my naps more than anything else about my former single life. Naps have been replaced with espresso shots. Luckily, I am engaged to a coffeehouse owner. Unluckily, coffee is not as good as naps.

There is NOTHING wrong with my love of napping. Napping is healthy. Researchers have found that naps reduce stress, increase productivity and alertness, are good for the heart and boost creativity. We are actually one of the only nations that do not encourage nap breaks at work. In some countries, a man can be put to death if he skips a nap. True story.

Unfortunately, in our stinking country, naps become impossible to take at some point in our lives. And I am at that point. There is just too much to do. There are not enough hours in a day. Even if Amy took all the kids out of the house and forbade me from stepping foot in The Buzz, I could not nap. I would look at the pile of work for my writing jobs that keeps getting larger and decide against a nap in order to work on it. If Amy took my work out of the house, I would grab the mop and broom and clean, rationalizing that if I have a few minutes work free I should do my part to keep the house tidy. If Amy hired a cleaning crew, I would realize I do not spend enough time with my dog anymore and take her on a long walk. And so on. I still love to nap. There is just no time to indulge this love.

What Amy could never accomplishment, her kids found a way to.

The Overnight Family Man

Her daughter threw up on October 15 and spent the night suffering through a 24-hour stomach bug. Her son caught it on October 17. It was passed to me on October 20. Amy had baked me a cake. I had two hockey tickets and was excited to be taking her son to his first ever game. And we had a babysitter the following night so we could spend an evening out alone … err… alone with Ben. It was set to be a great birthday weekend.

It was hell.

My birthday night was one of the worst evenings of my life! I threw up for five straight hours. I don't mean I threw up, tossed and turned in bed for an hour, threw up again, and so on for five hours. I mean that for FIVE STRAIGHT HOURS my head was in a bucket! It was hell! This was not a normal stomach bug. This was a children's virus passed on to an adult!

It felt like a demon was being forced out of my stomach! I didn't need a doctor; I needed a priest! The walls shook as my stomach emptied, my vomiting turned to dry heaving, and I screamed in pain as my insides tried to force themselves out of my mouth. I lost seven pounds that night!

Every situation has a silver lining, though, right?

For starters, when I woke up in the morning I found my missing abdomen muscles.

Plus, I was 100 percent too weak to work. So I had to lie in bed all day resting.

Yes, I got to take a nap. And, yes, despite being ill, it felt fantastic.

I got my birthday wish.

Thanks kids!

On a side note: This was not the first birthday I spent throwing up. It was, however, the first time I ever threw up on my birthday and did not mutter the famous words, "I promise I will never drink again."

11-13-11
Facebook Update

Ben learned to roll over this past week and I am NOT happy about it. I had Ben on my lap and my computer on the arm of my couch. I had been working like this ever since Ben was born. Then,

Ben decided to try to roll off my legs. If he succeeded, he would have rolled onto the floor. I quickly reacted and grabbed him. In the process, however, my arm bumped into my computer and knocked it onto the floor. Somehow that drop damaged my hard-drive. No, I am not going to brag when Ben hits development landmarks. Instead, I am going to mourn. As he develops, apparently my life gets tougher.

11-15-11
Facebook Update:
My son sucks. Four months old this week and still no eyebrows. WTF?!

12-2-11
My Broken Heart
My dog breaks my heart a little bit more each day.

Once I got engaged to Amy and accepted her children as my own, Habit dropped three spots on my list of priorities. It was hard to find time to spend with Habit. Often, the only time I could find for her at all was a 30-minute evening walk. Once Ben was born, she dropped another spot on my priority list. However, I remained her number one priority. I remained her entire world.

Once Ben was born, the only regular time I had for her – our walks – even disappeared. I now simply open the sliding glass door and let her walk around for a few hours for exercise … without me.

She struggled with the move initially, and then seemed to settle in. But now that I can barely find any time for her, her anxiety has returned. She cries and barks the day away.

I tried everything to calm her down. The veterinarian said it was normal; it was separation anxiety and that I should treat it with valium; yes, they actually prescribe dogs valium. That didn't work. Neither did Benadryl, which I was told would help her sleep, or a host of other medications. Each night I would drug her. Each night I would come close to breaking down in tears; the guilt that I was trying to drug away my dog's love for me was overwhelming. I would wrap the medication in a piece of bread and feed it to her and promise her that everything would work out, that I would find a way to incorporate her back into my life.

It was all a lie. And she knew it. Drugged and all, she barked the night away. No, she cried the night away.

I often see Facebook photos of my friends cuddled up on their bed with their dog and children and I get jealous. That is what I want for good ol' Habit. Habit deserves that type of life. She earned it by providing me with a lifetime of love. Unfortunately, that life is impossible to provide to Habit. I have three children, a writing career and a coffeehouse. It is hard to find time for a dog. I still sit with her and work late at night in the dog room, but because I am so busy I cannot give her the full attention she craves.

The saddest part of this story is that Habit's crying recently completely stopped. It means that she has either accepted her loneliness or she forgot how much time we used to spend together. I know it is selfish of me to write this – I hope when Habit's time comes it is not sudden. I don't want her to suffer, but I want 24 hours notice. I want to be able to allow her to sleep at my feet one last time so she can remember what life was once like. I don't want her current life to be her final memory.

Habit deserves better than this. Her only crime is loving me.

Unfortunately, I can't give her any better anymore ... and it breaks my heart.

12-5-11

Facebook Update:

I found fatherhood much easier before this little snot bucket could roll across floors.

12-9-11

It's My Book And I'll Cry If I Want To

I was warned, but I did not believe it.

While Amy was still pregnant, a friend of mine and father of three told me that the toughest thing about having a new baby is the tendinitis of the elbow I would develop.

He explained that women have hips that double as natural resting places for babies. Most men, on the other hand, are devoid of hips, which means when we hold babies we use only arm strength to do so.

I scoffed at him. It didn't matter that I already suffered from elbow tendonitis from time to time. I did not believe that holding a small baby would incur constant pain in my elbow.

For the first few months of Ben's life, I was capable of holding Ben for as long as it took without any problem. Then ... he turned the BIG TWO... as in two months old.

Three things happened when he turned two:

1. He became more aware of his surroundings. Everything began to amaze him. All he wanted to do was watch the world and soak in everything he saw.

2. His neck finally developed strong enough muscles to hold up his head. He went from bobble head to sturdy head, which meant that he was no longer dependent on me or Amy to hold his head still when something cool was occurring.

3. Both one and two meant that his sleeping time decreased. Prior to turning two months old, he slept for 20 hours a day, which is why holding him was so easy. I would only have to carry him around for a few minutes, he would fall asleep, and I would then lay him in his basinet to sleep for the next few hours. There was never an opportunity for him to ruin my elbow. But when he had a reason to stay awake – seeing the world – he did so.

That still doesn't seem like a reason for my arm to hurt. Why does it hurt my arm to sit him in my lap while he watches the world? Because he won't let me sit ... EVER! It's as though my pants and shirt pockets have rocks in them! Every time I sit down –placing him in my lap or on my chest he FREAKS THE HELL OUT! He starts screaming like he is having flashbacks of his circumcision.

Whenever he is awake and wants me to hold him, I need to stand the entire time, whether it is for a minute, an hour or three hours. When he hit this period in his life, I began to feel the first twinges of pain in my elbow. But, it was not that bad. Then ... then he turned four months old and teething began! *cue ominous music*

The pain he is experiencing must be unbearable because my sweet baby who once only cried when he peed his diaper (every time

… you would swear he has gonorrhea) and when I sat down with him, began to cry whenever he was awake. It is not so much a cry as a blood curdling shriek, the kind that gives you goose bumps. (A dentist told Amy and me that teething is so painful that it would drive an adult crazy.) If he is awake, he is in pain, which means he wants to be held … AT ALL TIMES. Since I can't sit down with him, I find myself standing most of the day, bopping up and down to try to calm him.

Oh yeah … did I mention that he is getting BIG! My tiny six-pound baby now weighs over 17 pounds. Seventeen pounds is not heavy. I curl more than three times that (yes, I am bragging). But, holding 17 pounds for up to three hours at a time multiple times a day has officially destroyed my elbow. This past Friday I must have held him for a total of 12 hours throughout the day. That is not an exaggeration.

The pain in my elbow got so bad that I had to ice it on Saturday.

When my journey into fatherhood began, one of my biggest fears was becoming the out of shape father, that finding time for the gym would become impossible. I still find time. (I have to go to the gym at 10 p.m. or later when everyone in the house is asleep, but I get to go.) It turned out the biggest detriment to my physical wellbeing is a 17-pound snot bucket who I love.

I have written over and over again throughout this past year, but it holds as true today as it did the first time – BEING A FATHER IS HARD!

And to all the women reading this who are saying to themselves, "Oh stop! Try carrying the baby around for 10 months! Stop complaining," I say, go write your own book! This is mine and I can cry if I want to!

12-16-11
My Son's Girlie Blanket

My son has a pink blanket that he loves and it is killing me!

The blanket is his favorite thing in the world. When he is crying, all I have to do is hand it to him and he is instantly appeased. No matter the problem, whether his stomach hurts from gas or his mouth hurts from to teething, whether he is hungry and impatiently waiting for us to prepare his bottle or whether he is in one of those overly tired yet cannot seem to figure out how to fall asleep moods, if I hand him that damn pink fluffy blanket, he is happy within seconds. He pulls it up to his face and rubs it against his cheek like he is in heaven ... and it bothers me.

The reason he has a pink blanket is because as the third child he is the "hand-me-down" child. Almost everything he owns was once owned by his big brother or sister. The blanket was his sister's. It is the warmest baby-sized blanket we own so when the cold spell hit Tampa last week it was the most logical blanket to cover him with when we went outside, no matter the color. He instantly took to it and cooed in ecstasy when we placed it over him. We immediately knew it would become his security blanket, the one he would carry with him throughout his toddler years.

It doesn't bother me because it is pink. I am not one of those overly macho fathers who needs everything his son wears to be blue and with a sports team emblem on it. Ben can wear pink and any other color designated as "girly" from now until the end of time for all I care. He can play with dolls instead of video games and dance instead of playing football. None of that bothers me. Hell, my favorite toy when I was a little kid was a Wonder Woman doll that I carried with me everywhere. My parents tried desperately to break me of the habit by buying me more masculine dolls, such as a Muhammad Ali doll. Nothing took like that Wonder Woman doll. I loved it. And I turned out fine ... *insert numerous jokes at my expense here.*

What bothers me about the blanket is not its feminine connotation. It's that I have no sentimental attachment to it while Amy does.

When Amy sees him with the blanket, she sighs a happy sigh and reminisces about how the blanket came into her possession and about the first time she laid it on her daughter. She has mental and real photographs of her daughter covered with that blanket as a baby. So many landmark moments in her daughter's early infancy include that blanket. To see her new baby covered in it elicits joy in Amy.

I don't share any of those memories because I was not around for her daughter's baby-hood. When Amy evokes those recollections, I just sit their quietly.

And that is the case with everything of Ben's. When we dress Ben in his New York Met's jersey, Amy comments how cute her 6-year-old son looked in it when he was a baby. When he plays with his toys, Amy tells me which toy was her son's favorite and which was her daughter's. When he sits in his highchair and smears baby food all over his face, she laughs, looks at the other two kids and tells them they used to do the same thing. And so on.

I feel gypped.

I realize that in time I will have my own memories of each of these toys but it is not the same. For the first time since I have become a part of Amy's family, I feel like I'm on the outside looking in. They have memories I can never share; it is a subtle reminder that no matter how much I love them and see them as my own, they are not mine. They come from another man.

Oddly enough, that is not my major issue with Ben's blanket, his clothes, toys and other accessories. I also feel like I have been gypped out of spoiling my son.

I see some of my friends who just had their first babies spoiling them rotten. They bring their child a new toy every day. They buy new shirts with cheesy slogans like, "Daddy's Little Boy" and "My Father Rocks" and so on.

I can't do any of that because Ben already has everything. Buying him new clothes and toys when he already has handed down to him than we know what to do with seems ridiculous and a waste of money. Why would I buy him a stuffed animal when we have two boxes full of them? Why buy him a shirt with a cheesy slogan when he has doubles on most of the slogans? And why buy him a new blanket when he already has one he loves? It would be financially irresponsible for me to spoil him with presents. We could win the lottery tomorrow and it wouldn't change my attitude on spending. As most people with three children would say, there is no such thing as financial stability when you have three mouths to feed, three bodies to clothe and three minds to put through college. Reckless spending should not exist when you have a large family and buying unneeded toys is reckless.

I have not yet bought my son a single present. And it bothers me no matter how right I know I am in abstaining.

I know how odd that is, to be bothered as much by not being

able to buy my son toys as being reminded that my other two children are not really my own. However, the thought that they are not my children always quickly subsides. They are mine. I am their father. But the fact that I will never have memories of spoiling a baby never escapes me.

Is it worth it? Of course. I gave up those memories in exchange for two children I love.

But still ... it kind of sucks.

12-22-11
Facebook Update:
I have come to the conclusion that it is useless. I will never find clothes that fit Ben. They do not make five-month clothes for babies with 12-month heads.

12-25-11
Facebook Update:
I didn't have to put anything together this year. Merry Christmas to me!

12-25-11
Facebook Update:
I would like to thank Santa for the bottle of Dewers and late night NBA tonight. Santa, you have proven that you are more powerful than Jesus, so if anyone can make my son a Nets fan AND bring the Nets a title in my lifetime, it is you. Make it happen! And if you can get me five front row seats to the clinching game for me, my brother, dad and my sons, all the better.

12-30-11
Your Children Stink!
Apparently, Christmas brings out the BS in almost everyone.

Late Christmas Day eve, I was surfing Facebook to see photographs of what my family up north did on Christmas and could not help but to laugh out loud at some of my friends' updates.

"Just a perfect Christmas morning," wrote one, his nose probably growing with each letter he struck on his keyboard.

"I am so blessed to have had such a perfect day with my

children," commented another lying friend.

"I got everything I wanted on Christmas morning - angels for children," a third had the gall to write.

And so on.

Any honest person with children has probably rolled his or her eyes by now. The reason is – there is no such thing as a "sitcom" Christmas morning in real life. No Christmas is perfect. They are hectic, hectic, HECTIC and imperfect in every way.

My two years as a father on Christmas morning and my many friends with children have taught me that all young children fall into one of the following categories:

1. The overwhelmed: The many presents and the thought that Santa Claus visited their home just hours earlier becomes too much for them to handle and at some point late in the morning they have a complete breakdown and tantrum themselves to sleep.

2. The underwhelmed: Either they did not get what they want or the toy they craved for so long let them down for a number of reasons. These children fall into a funk and spend the rest of the day depressed, asking when their birthday is and how long it is until next Christmas, hoping that one of those holidays will prove more fulfilling.

3. The spoiled: All the presents in the world cannot appease these children. They throw tantrums for more presents even after they opened 100 and received everything they wanted.

4. The distracted: As you wait anxiously for them to rip the wrapping paper off each of their presents and shriek in glee at what they find, they get stalled on the first present they open. They are so excited to receive it that they immediately begin playing with it and forget they have more to open.

5. My children fall into categories 1 and 4.

My 3-year-old stepdaughter doesn't so much care about what she was gets as much as she does opening the presents; ripping wrapping paper off a box brings her pure joy. Knowing this, Amy and I bought her numerous small presents rather than a few large ones. This year, because she now has my family, Amy's family and Amy's ex-husband's family ALL buying her presents with this in mind, she had enough boxes to rebuild the Berlin Wall. Halfway through her present-opening spree, Amy had to halt her before her small toys got lost in a swamp of wrapping paper and were accidently thrown away. She did not take kindly to the timeout and launched into yet another epic tantrum. Merry Christmas!

My 6-year old stepson received a very special gift – the very desk I used as a kid in my bedroom. My grandfather made the desk by hand for me when I was around 6 years old and it has been collecting dusk in my parents' attic for decades.

My stepson has needed a desk for some time to fit his growing collection of homemade books. It is the greatest compliment he has ever given me. He knows I am a writer so he wants to write books of his own to impress me. The books are cute – five pieces of paper stapled together with a simple sentence such as, "I love mac and cheese" written on each page. They are also frustrating, as we find them scattered throughout the house at all times. He makes at least one a day, sometimes more.

When Amy mentioned we should get him a desk for Christmas to store all his books and book-making supplies, I immediately called my father and asked him to ship my old desk down to me. Passing on the desk my late-grandfather made for me felt great. Amy, however, was a bit nervous for me. She was scared he would blow right by the desk and not care about it, breaking my heart. Instead, the opposite occurred. It was the first thing he saw and he loved it so much that he immediately sat at it and began making a new book. No matter how much we pled with him to finish opening his presents, he would not budge until he was done writing a book about his new desk while sitting at his new desk.

That was our Christmas morning ... one kid throwing

tantrums because she wanted to open presents as fast as she could and one who did not want to open anything. Then there was our third, Ben, who is teething so badly that his drool is becoming an issue. Holding him is like trying to grip a Vaseline-covered watermelon in a pool. Amy and I passed him back and forth so many times that you'd have sworn he was a hot potato in a nursery school game. We weren't avoiding holding him because we were scared we were going to drop him but because ... well ... he was gross.

That is as perfect as Christmas' gets. Do not fall for any parent's "My Christmas was perfect" BS. Trust me. Each of my friends who posted about their perfect Christmases has children who are booger eating spazoids just like mine. There is no way that those disgusting monsters offered anything close to perfection. That is not meant to be disrespectful to my friends' children or my children. ALL children are booger eating spazoids. We love them ... but they are booger eating spazoids nonetheless.

With ALL that said, the hectic atmosphere that is Christmas with children is all worth it because each Christmas does offer a worthy memory or memories that do stay with you for all time. Last Christmas was my first with my new family. This year was not only my first with my newborn biological son, but also offered other intangibles, such as giving my stepson my childhood desk and hearing Ben's first word. Yes, you read that correctly. Ben spoke!

While the children were opening presents, Amy told one of them that the present they were opening came from "Paul's daddy" and Ben immediately blurted out, "Daddy." It was as clear as day. Both Amy and I heard it. There was NO mistaking what he said.

True... he is only five months old so chances are that it was mere babble, Ben mimicking Amy's last word and luckily doing so in perfect fashion. There is no way any son of mine is a baby genius and speaking at five months old would toss him into that category. The fact that he did not repeat the word again despite our constant egging proves that the mimicking theory is probably true. Nonetheless, I will ignore scientific protocol on this occasion and go with the first word theory. Hell, if my friends can claim that their children are perfect, I can remember this Christmas as the day my son chose to say "Daddy" for his first word.

1-4-12
Facebook Update:
I would like every parent with one or two sets of grandparents living nearby to go F themselves and whenever you feel like complaining about how hard your day was because of your kids, remember you have grandparents to help and then F yourself again. That is all.

1-5-12
Facebook Update:
Wait ... I just realized something ... I have become a stay-at-home dad! When and how did this happen? Amy and I never had a sit down discussion about this ... but it happened!

1-6-12:
I'm Better Than Luke Skywalker
Christopher Columbus ... considered one of the bravest men in the history of the world for daring to prove the naysayers wrong by sailing around the world.

Neil Armstrong ... considered one of the bravest men in the history of the world for daring to become the first man on the moon.

Luke Skywalker ... considered one of the bravest men in the history of the universe for daring to take on Darth Vader after both Yoda and Obi Won Kenobi said he was not ready.

Paul Guzzo ... considered one of the bravest men in the history of the world, universe, heaven and hell for daring to take a five-month old baby to see a movie.

Admit it; my accomplishment is FAR more impressive than the other members of that list!

Why? Why would I attempt such a feat? Because of two of the most nightmarishly paired words in the parental dictionary – Winter Break!

My 6-year-old stepson was off from school for two weeks and we are a two-income family. Because Amy is always at the coffeehouse where he can disrupt costumers and I work from home where he can only disrupt me, I pulled the figurative short straw and had to entertain him throughout the break. I tried to find time for him – I took him on a daylong ride on the trolley, Christmas shopping for his mother, the aquarium, the park and for pizza on a few occasions

– but I also had to work. During my working time, he would go stir crazy, bouncing off walls as only a 6-year-old trapped inside a house all day can.

After two straight all day work days during his second week of break, he came down with a case of the "ants in pants," as my mother used to call it. He sat in the living room with me as I tried to work, TRY being the key word, rolling around the floor, doing handstands on the couch, and sometimes just pretending to fry like bacon. Or at least I hope he was pretending to fry like bacon, otherwise I have NO idea what he was doing.

Come day three, though I had a lot of work to do, I HAD to get him out of the house. But it was raining. What could I do?

DING DING DING! Take him see the new Muppets movie, I decided! It would fill time and it was a movie we would both enjoy. I thought it was a brilliant idea. No one else agreed. The reason being, because I had to take five-month-old Ben with us as well.

Amy told me that there was no way Ben would make it through the entire film. He would get antsy, hungry, poop his pants, etc. – all issues that would end up with him crying to the point that I would have to drag him from the theatre until he was calm. Because my stepson is only 6, he would have to leave with me. Amy promised that the day would end with both Ben and my stepson crying, the latter doing so because he had to miss the end of the movie.

I scoffed at her! I know my son, I thought, and he is always calm when watching colorful images flashing on the television screen. With colorful images flashing on a giant movie screen, I was sure he would sit still in a catatonic state while staring in awe of the enormous Muppets.

To make a fun day out of it, we took the trolley to Ybor City, where we would catch the movie. While making small talk with a family on the streetcar, I mentioned I was taking the boys to see a movie and they stared at me like I had just told them I was thinking of wearing a Dallas Cowboys jersey in downtown Philadelphia.

"First day on the job," asked the wife/mother, mocking what she thought was my poor decision making skills as a father. "There is no way a five-month-old can make it through a movie."

I told her I was confident in my boy. She replied that she

wished she had milk to drink so she could spit it out her nose as she laughed at me (Not true at all, but let's pretend that she did say that), but I was undeterred.

We then stopped for pizza in Ybor and our waitress had the same reaction to my plan as did Amy and the trolley family.

"I have some old cheese you can eat while you're at it. That's as good an idea as taking a baby to a movie" she joked. I stared at her stone faced and told her not to quit her day job. (Again, not true. I faked a laugh, but let's pretend I had the courage to call her on her bad joke.) However, I would not be deterred. I took my five-month-old son to the movie anyway.

And guess what.........HE MADE IT THROUGH THE ENTIRE FILM! IN YOUR FACE YOU UNFUNNY STRANGERS!

You are DYING to know how he did it, correct? It was easy – I know my son:

1. We sat in the very back of the theatre so I could stand up as I held him without impairing anyone's view. Whenever he began to get antsy, I stood up with him and he calmed down.

2. I brought my diaper bag with the fold out changing table so I could change him when he peed. True, I may have lucked out that he did not poop but I think it had less to do with luck and more to do with me whispering in his ear throughout the movie, "No poop! No poop! No poop!"

3. I nuked a bottle to a boil at the pizza place. Ben is a bit of an eating priss. His bottles HAVE to be warm. If they are not, he spits the formula out and howls in anger until it is heated. So I fed him at the pizza place and then boiled a second bottle of formula, knowing it would cool down yet still be warm when he was hungry again in the middle of the movie.

4. I placed my jacket on an empty seat near the theatre's entrance to save the seat. This was my most brilliant

move.

Ben fell asleep about 30 minutes into the movie. When he woke up and freaked out as most baby's do when they wake because they are either hungry, peed their diaper or are confused as to where they are, I rushed him into the entrance hallway, which is always lit up, and placed my stepson in the seat where my jacket was placed so I could calm Ben while keeping an eye on him. I changed Ben on the diaper's bag fold out table, fed him the formula that was at the perfect temperature, and then calmed him by walking in circles with him, never taking one eye off my stepson, who did not have to miss a second of the movie.

All three of us then returned to our seats in the back and made it through the rest of the movie without an incident. I even think that Ben danced in my lap during the finale song.

I did good. No ... I did great.

When I bragged to Amy later that day of my success, she scoffed at my celebratory attitude.

"All luck," she said. "Just a perfect storm."

Maybe so ... or maybe ... just maybe ... I am the greatest father of all time.

1-9-11
Facebook Update:
I am trying to perfect this stay-at-home/work-from-home dad hybrid. Busy day, praying to Tebow that Ben is good and naps properly and stops making that disgusting horse noise when he slobbers for hours on end!

1-10-11
Facebook Update:
I took good ol' Habit on a one mile walk. Getting a bit of a limp, but the old dog still made it and walked briskly.

1-13-11
Facebook Update:
For those wondering when Amy and I are getting married ... don't hold your breath. We decided that spending money on a

wedding right now is silly and if we do City Hall we will never have a wedding, so we are waiting until the time is right – probably years from now. Ben is more binding than a wedding ring anyway. Sorry to all you mooches who wanted open bar.

1-27-11
I Am Mom

"I feel for you," said the elderly employee at Kinko's as he held the door for me so I could manage carrying a sleeping Ben in his car seat, the diaper bag and my briefcase. "My wife passed away shortly after our baby was born and I had to raise him on my own."

Huh? I thought, unsure why he was confiding such a personal memory to me as I walked through the door.

"When did your wife pass?" he asked.

"My wife is not dead," I replied, even more confused.

Actually, I wanted to explain that Amy and I are not really married because we cannot seem to find the time or the extra cash to plan a decent wedding but do not care because the baby is more binding than a wedding ring. I always want to explain that to people, but it is such a mouthful that I just call Amy my wife. Considering how confusing our conversation was already, I thought trying to explain my marital situation would just make it all the more perplexing.

"Oh," he said, "well, I still know how tough it is to be a single father."

I had not yet caught on to why we were having this conversation, so I replied, "Single? No. We're still together."

He opened his mouth but nothing came out. It was his turn to be confused ... very confused.

While he said nothing, his eyes told me everything – he was staring at my briefcase.

I have visited that Kinko's at least once, sometimes twice, a week for the past few years. The elderly employee almost always seems to be scheduled during my visits, so he knows I have a job. That is why he was so confused. Every time the elderly employee has seen me since Ben was born, I have had him in tow. If I have a "wife" and a job, why am I always with the baby?

The elderly Kinko's employee is not alone in his confusion.

I take Ben to the doctor to get his regular checkups. On my third visit I mentioned that my wife (again, easier to call her my wife) wanted me to ask some questions about Ben's poor sleeping habits. The nurse replied, "Your wife? His mom?" as though the news that Ben had a living or active mother was shocking. I have since realized that I am always the ONLY father who is alone with a baby at the pediatrician's office. Either mothers or mothers and fathers seem to take babies to the doctor. It never seems that ONLY a father does such a task.

I also can't remember a trip to the bank when someone in line hasn't pointed to Ben and asked, "Have him for the day, huh?" When I tell them I have him every day, they seem shocked. I get the question so often that one of the bank's regular tellers recently answered for me, blurting out, "Today? They are inseparable!"

In fact, we are so inseparable that when I recently made a rare trip to the grocery store without him, multiple employees asked me where he was. It was the first time in months they had seen me without him and they were worried that meant he was sick.

Because we are together so often, many of the people I see on a regular basis now call me "Mom." Obviously they don't do so because I am a woman, but because the parent who usually spends the daytime hours with a baby is the mom. And in a way, they are right. I am the daytime mom. Mothers are usually the parent who babies seek when they need comforting. During the day, when Ben is in need of love, he wants me. On a recent occasion, his belly ached and, to steal a phrase from my mother, he was "screaming bloody murder." I had to make a quick run to the grocery store for The Buzz (the trip in which I was minus Ben) and Amy was temporarily caring for him on a rare daytime occasion. She could not get him to stop crying. As soon as I returned, I grabbed him, he buried his head in my chest and fell asleep. A woman with whom Amy was talking jokingly said, "Aw, he missed his mom."

There have been numerous occasions in which I have asked a friend to hold him while I tend to a chore, such as sending a quick email or making a quick call. When Ben gets fussy, my friends have mentioned that just the sound of my voice when I yell to him, "Be right back Ben," from across the room has calmed him. And when he cries in the car, he calms when I sing to him.

If I am "mom," does that make Amy dad? In a way, that is also correct. Because I am with Ben so often, he does not ever completely miss me. But when he sees Amy, he dances for joy. I have often heard mothers lament that they get jealous of their husbands due to the fact that children are usually more excited to see the father than the mother because the father is usually gone more than the mother; distance makes the heart grow fonder. I now understand that feeling. I do sometimes get jealous of how excited Ben gets when he sees Amy.

Mom ... it is a nickname I have come to accept yet have found hard to accept.

While I embrace the role and consider myself lucky to be able to be the rare man who gets to watch his baby boy grow up; while I love that I am the one teaching him to crawl and teaching him to talk; while I get goose bumps when crying Ben buries his head in my chest for comfort; and while I laugh at the fact that I lecture others on how to hold my baby, how hot to make his bottle or how to properly burp him (facts that moms, not dads, usually know), part of me also hates to be called "mom." I sometimes find it demeaning. Whenever people realize that I am the stay-at-home-dad, I feel the need to somehow slip into the conversation that I have a job and that I work from home. I feel that people must think I am unemployed if I am a stay-at-home dad and I feel that emasculates me in a way. The stereotype says that men work in the fields and women stay home and cook and clean.

Amy is also a bit offended at times when I am called mom. She thinks other women look down upon her for choosing to work rather than stay at home with her newborn baby. She has also fallen victim to the stereotype.

The truth is that stereotype is bullshit. Norman Rockwell is dead. Families have to do what works best for them, not society's stereotypes. It is easier for me to work with Ben than it is for Amy because I work from home. And if I was not working and Amy alone was paying the bills, so be it. While I may never have the self-confidence to fully embrace my role, I can accept it and accept that I am lucky to be a "daytime mom."

When Amy comes home from work, she takes on all motherly roles to Ben and the other children. And just as Ben only wants me to comfort him during the day, because he is accustomed to Amy being "mom" at night, she is the only one he wants in the evening hours. When the sun goes down, only Amy can soothe him.

In our family, there is no real mom or dad. Mom and dad are names only, not roles. In our household, there are just two parents who love their kids.

That is the new American family.

2-3-11
Facebook Update:

I will dedicate my life to the church if Tebow could grant me just two hours of time to actually get some work done today! For the love of Tebow, I have worked just a few hours in the past two weeks!

2-3-12
I'm Late For A Very Important Date!

If I am Speedy Gonzales, my family is his cousin, Slowpoke Rodriguez.

When I was a child, if there was one GIANT "No-No" in our house, it was being late. My mother would NEVER allow it.

If we had to be at an event at 3 p.m. that was 15 minutes away, she had all three kids ready and waiting on the porch by 2 p.m. She knew that if you give kids the slightest window of opportunity to make you late, they will find it – they will spill juice on their shirts; hide behind a chair so not to be found, thinking it is a funny game; start watching a television show and throw a tantrum that they want to see the end, squirming so much that it takes 15 minutes to drag them from the room; or spill a bottle of crazy glue on the floor, step in it and be stuck to the floor like a man in a hardhat glued to a construction beam.

Our porch had ZERO distractions. It was screened in, so we could not run around outside. It had no toys, television or radio. All it had was three chairs for us to sit in. And that is what we did. If our mom said to be ready and sitting on that porch by 2 p.m., we were on the porch. Nothing, and I mean NOTHING scared us more than being the reason we were late for an affair. My mom turned from Joan Clever to Sam Kinison if we were one second late. She was the rabbit from Alice in Wonderland!

That "never be late" attitude has shaped my life perhaps more than anything else my parents instilled upon me. As a child in grade school, while teachers would yell at other students to hurry up, stop screwing around and finish their work, they would yell at me to slow down and take my time. I always felt like I had to GO GO GO so I could be the first one done; I did not want to be late! I received good grades as a kid – my urgency did not come at the cost of getting the wrong answers. Teachers wanted me to slow down because it worried them that I was so stressed out about getting done on time.

This urgency is what made journalism the perfect career for me. Writing is primarily about stringing words together into easy-to-read descriptive sentences, but it is also about doing so in a timely fashion. One of the first questions asked on any writing job interview revolves around one's ability to meet a deadline. The press cannot wait for Slow Poke Rodriguez!

Considering my mother turned me into a deadline-oriented monster, it is a bit ironic that I have joined the slowest … family … ever …

Amy has many great qualities. She is drop dead gorgeous. She can fix just about anything – plumbing, electrical problems, etc. – which is great considering I cannot even fix a sandwich. She is also a great cook, a brilliant businesswoman, hardworking, dedicated, a loving mother … have I buttered her up enough before I mention her negative quality? … She is also the SLOWEST WOMAN I HAVE EVER MET.

She is not slow as in she walks and moves slowly; she is slow in a way that she can know all day long that we need to leave by 1 p.m. to get to where we need. Yet, at 12:55 she will jump in the shower and then have a long list of things she realizes she needed to do before we leave. I love Amy so much but this quality drives me insane.

And her kids have inherited it. They are SOOOOOO pokie!

I can tell the 6-year-old to put on his shoes a million times. Each time I tell him, he will jump up from his chair to do it, but something always distracts him along the way – a cartoon, a toy, a crumb, etc. When it is time to leave, not only will he still be barefoot, but he won't even know where his shoes are.

The 3-year-old is pokie in a different manner – she is just plain stubborn. As we are walking out the door, she will decide she does not like the outfit that her mom picked out for her and scream that she wants to change. If we don't give in, she will tantrum and we will be late. If we give in and let her change, as we open the door to leave, she will decide she wants to wear the original outfit. She is like that with shoes, hair ties and even whatever she is drinking – she wants apple juice, no water, no apple juice, and so on.

So, with ALL that said, one of my biggest concerns in regard to Ben has been whether or not he will be slow and pokie. I need at least one more ally on my team! Amy said I have no chance, that all kids are slow, that my siblings and I were freaks of nature because we had a sense of urgency as kids, and that she is not slow at all, that I am just crazy.

She may be right, but last week I tried to begin to instill some of my craziness onto Ben. Whenever I had to leave the house, I would repeat to him, "We're in a rush! We're in a rush! We're in a rush!" I was hoping that urgency reinforcement in infants works the same as positive reinforcement. It turns out that blood is thicker than enforcement. As I rushed out the door to my noon lunch meeting, he projectile vomited all over me. I quickly changed him and myself, and as I rushed out the door again, he pooped.

I was late.

2-13-11
Facebook Update:
My stepson has to write a three sentence report on an African American for African American month. I want him to write about Ray Parker Jr., the author of his favorite song - Ghostbusters - but mean Amy doesn't like the idea.

2-17-12
Facebook Update:
I would give up both testicles for one full day of work.

2-17-12
Darth Vader May Be A Better Dad Than Me
I felt like the worst father in the world. The first time my

stepson was bullied was partially my fault.

As a reward for good behavior at school, he was allowed to choose one prize from the toy chest in his kindergarten class. These toys are cheap five and dime trinkets, the kind that dentists used to give out (or perhaps they still do) to child patients. But to 5- and 6-year-old children, all toys are priceless, especially when he or she gets one and most of the class does not; it is a great bragging moment.

For my stepson, his big moment turned embarrassing. That day's options were two notepads, probably a total of a few inches in height and width. One had Hello Kitty on the cover and the other had *Star Wars*. My stepson chose Hello Kitty and the rest of the boys let him have it. They called him a girl over and over again. When I picked him up from school, he held back his tears as he told me the story; he was crushed. It was the first time in his life that he had been picked on by his peers.

I told him that he shouldn't care what other kids think about him and that he should continue doing what makes him happy. I explained that when I was his age my favorite toy was a Wonder Woman doll and I turned out fine. Be an individual, I explained, not a conformist just to have friends. I knew that those words went in one ear and out the other. All little kids just want is to fit in rather than be individuals or, as individuals are called in school, outcasts. Nevertheless, I continued with my "parenting."

"Why did you choose the Hello Kitty notebook?" I asked.

"Because it's the only one I recognized," he said. "I didn't know what *Star Wars* was."

Oof! It felt like I was punched in the stomach. I am supposed to be raising him, molding him into a man, and he did not know *Star Wars*. I felt like I had failed him. We have all six DVDs at the house and I had not found any time to introduce him to the films. He knew Hello Kitty because Amy has taken time to introduce it to our 3-year-old. Amy had done her job as a mother. I had not done mine as a father.

Not only is *Star Wars* crucial to any boy's world in the same way as baseball, pro wrestling and dirt, but it was a MAJOR part of my childhood as well. I lived, breathed and ate *Star Wars* as a little boy, as did all boys back then. There are few if any other films that have transcended generations as *Star Wars* has. If ever there was anything for us to further bond over it is *Star Wars*. Yet, I could not find the time to spend with him watching the films. I have never been more disappointed in myself in my life. True, I have an excuse, well, two actually – a new business and new baby are consuming. However, the mark of a good parent is one who can always find equal time for his or her kids.

The day after his first bullying experience, we began our *Star Wars* bond. I started him with *Phantom Menace* (which some say is hypocrisy because I should start him with *A New Hope*, but I wanted him to watch them as George Lucas intended) and went from there. He fell in love with the movies immediately. Within two weeks he had made it all the way to *Empire Strikes Back* and I had watched most of each film with him, only missing parts when I needed rock Ben to sleep, feed him or change him. He asked me a million questions about the films – Why don't the good guys have two light sabers like the bad guy? How do you make a robot evil? Why did Darth Vader need to blow up a whole planet? And so on. (I wonder if he will ask me if it is creepy that Luke kisses his sister in *Empire* … God I hope not. Because it is and I don't want him to realize that Luke is just plain creepy for not seeming to care!)

Then, while watching TV together one Sunday evening, it happened! We saw an advertisement for the re-release of *Phantom Menace* … in 3D! It was hard to tell who was more excited for this news. We both jumped out of our seats and in unison exclaimed to the other – "Do you want to go?!" It was awesome!

And then … I ruined it.

Thinking I was being a good parent, I told him that we would see it on opening weekend – just the two of us; no baby and no girls, a real "man day" as he loves to call it – if he received all green marks in behavior during that school week. The teacher gives greens for good behavior, yellows for subpar and reds for bad. He rarely receives anything but greens so it seemed like a slam dunk way in which to reward him for being a well behaved student.

Perhaps the pressure was too much for him to handle because for the first time all year he received BACK-TO-BACK yellows! The first was for playing around during a fire drill and the second was for talking too much in class. I was devastated. I wanted to see the movie too! So, after he received the first yellow I decided to give him a second chance.

I told him if he could go the rest of the week without getting into trouble, we would go. I felt no reason to punish him for getting into trouble once.

Going to the movie seemed like a bigger lock, especially because he had off from school on Friday. He only needed to be good for three more days … and he still failed.

BUT, I gave him ONE MORE chance. I REALLY wanted to see the movie! If he could go one day … just ONE DAY … without fighting with his sister, I would take him. I know that sounds impossible, but we were spending that day at the State Fair! With all that fun, how could they fight?! Yes, I am still kind of new to this parenting thing.

He was good all day at the fair. Then, just five minutes after we returned home, he pinched his sister … RIGHT IN FRONT OF ME! I couldn't ignore it. I had to finally live up to my threat.

When I told him we were not going to see the movie that weekend and that there would be no fourth chance, he was devastated. He said all the other boys would be seeing it that weekend and were going to make fun of him. He told me he hated me. And he told me I smelled like poop. (Which is NOT true! B.O. maybe … but not poop!)

It is not the first time one of the children has hated me for putting my foot down. Usually it bounces right off of me. They are just kids. They don't really mean it. But this one hurt because he was earnestly crushed and I couldn't help but think it was my fault. He deserved to see the movie no matter how he behaved that week. It is not like he back talked to the teacher or got caught smoking in the boy's room. He was just acting like a little boy who was having too much fun at school. But I told him he had to get all greens and I told him he couldn't fight with his sister and I had to stick to my guns.

One of the lessons I learned early in my "family man" life is not to make veiled threats as a parent. If you tell your children they will lose something if they are bad you have to take it away if they misbehave or they will NEVER respect your threats of punishment. That is why you can't yell things such as "I will burn down Disney World if you don't stop fighting!" (People without kids are gasping that a parent would yell that while parents are nodding and smiling right now.) In fact, you can't even threaten not to take them to Disney. That is too big of a planned event to take away and you will cave and go. Instead, you have to say things like, "No candy at Disney!" Veiled threats will kill your street cred as a parent, which is why I could not take my stepson to the movie.

So I didn't get to see *Star Wars* in 3D last weekend. And I am mad!

I wonder how Darth Vader would have handled the situation if he had raised Luke.

2-21-11
Facebook Update:
I am stuck in traffic with a baby who pooped. Kill me.

2-24-12
The Day I Cut The Cord?
Dear Ben,

If you are reading this, it means it has been years since I originally penned it, which means you are probably old enough to know the truth:

The first time I left you with a babysitter was … … … one of the easiest things I have ever done! And I had a blast doing it!

Please don't take offense to that. You were seven months old at the time! We had no grandparents or other relatives to watch after you (If you are going to mention that your Uncle Pete lived around the corner, don't. Trust me, Uncle Pete was not going to babysit three kids) so the only way to leave you home was with a babysitter. It took a while to build up the courage to leave you with her, so for seven long months your mother and I had ZERO alone time when we went out. We either stayed home or lugged your big headed infant self around with us. (Sorry Ben, but you had a BIG head as a baby. I pray your body has caught up to it by now.)

For seven LOOOOOONG months, everywhere your mom and I went together included you, a stroller, a baby seat and a diaper bag. On occasion, we left your brother and sister with their paternal grandparents (their biological father's parents) for a few hours on a weekend afternoon and we would go out for lunch or a walk, but you were always with us. On one occasion, we thought it would be fun to have lunch at a restaurant on the beach. It would have been fun ... if you weren't screaming bloody murder the entire time! Ever since that painful day, I had been ready to leave you at home.

There were times during your first seven months of life that we would leave your brother and sister with a babysitter, but you still came with us. Your mom would tell people that she was ready to leave you at home with a sitter but we hadn't yet because I was not ready, because I was still too attached to not be with you. I am not sure why she felt fine fibbing like that, but I can assure you that she was 100 percent lying. Part of me thinks it was because she was not ready, so she used me as her cover.

The truth is, I was over being the man at the social event with the baby in his arm since you were a few months old. Don't misunderstand, you were an easy baby. Except for the beach incident, you never cried or tantrumed in public. You would just chill out and relax as you sat on my arm and held one arm around my neck. But it gets tiring having to talk about your baby all night. And that is all people wanted to talk about as long as you were with us. Making matters worse, even as a few-month old, you looked exactly like me, so people would often comment that I looked like a ventriloquist and you looked like my mini-me dummy. After six or seven times, that joke got real old.

Your mom was kind of right, however. While I was ready to leave you behind, I did not want to do it. I was more worried about your brother and sister, however, than you. They were not over-the-top jealous of you, the new baby, but there were small signs here and there, like when your brother got mad at me for calling you "buddy," which was my name for him, or when your sister tried to smother you in your sleep while she screamed, "I'm the baby! I'm the baby!" Ok, I made that last one up, but I will guess that your sister hasn't changed too much since she was 3 years old so part of you believed that could have been possible. Anyway, your siblings were very close with their babysitter, so close that when your sister was asked who she wanted to invite to her third birthday party she listed her sitter second. I was worried that since the sitter would have had to pay extra attention to you because you were a baby that your brother and sister would think you "stole" their friend and hold it against you. I didn't want to stir the pot.

But, after seven months of dragging you everywhere, I finally said jealousy be damned and left you behind.

In the days leading up to that big moment, parent after parent told me that it would be the hardest thing I had ever done. I would explain that I had left your siblings home dozens of times, but I was told a baby is different. Plus, people said that I was trained on leaving your siblings behind before I fell in love with them, which made it easier.

Guess what? Yeah, you already know – it WAS NOT hard.

The sitter showed up, I gave her the instructions on when you eat and go to bed and how you like your bottle slightly warmed because you are a giant pansy. (Yes, I really did say that to her. Seriously dude, you needed your bottle to be the exact right temperature! You were SO high maintenance when it came to eating!) I then kissed your brother and sister goodbye, hugged you tight, kissed you a dozen times (I'm not an animal. I may not have missed you, but I felt bad leaving you) and then walked out the door. The moment I climbed in the car, I felt lighter than I had in months. It was the first time since you were born that I didn't have to carry a cache of baby supplies when I was with your mom! And we drove away. We both mentioned to the other how we felt guilty that it was so easy to leave you home. That guilt did not last long.

Your mom and I had so much fun! We went to a party. We went to a film fest opening night celebration. We went to a bar! We had drinks! We laughed! We talked about anything but kids! It was the most fun we'd had together in a long time. Your mom called the sitter two or three times to check on the house, but that is normal procedure when you leave your kids with a sitter, whether it is the first or 100th time.

Look Ben, we loved you and still do. Don't take it personal. People in love like your mom and me need some alone time sooner or later. Trust me. You'll have kids one day too and when you do, you will also experience that taste of rediscovered freedom and love it.

I will always love you and will always be there for you ... but I will also always need a little alone time out on the town with your mom. That actually works out for you – it leaves our house open for parties when we go out. Of course, if you have a party, I'll punish you by spreading a rumor that you sit while you pee. Seriously dude. Don't test me.

Love,
Your dad

P.S. If your body never grew to match your head, sorry about that big head joke. It looks good on you Ben. I swear.

3-2-12
Ben's Monumental Week

I feel like my moment was stolen from me.

My career has been put on the backburner. That is not to say it is suffering; I find the time to do what I need to do, but that time is only when there is nothing else to do for someone else in the house. While it bothers me to some extent that my career is the least important thing in my house, I live with it because I have realized how lucky I am to be able to spend so much time with Ben. Most fathers miss the infant years of their children's life and never get to experience their children's firsts. I am right on the frontline of it all and have been looking forward to celebrating all of Ben's milestones with him.

Then, it was stolen from me.

My stepdaughter was sick on Monday, which meant I had to work at The Buzz so Amy could stay home and tend to her; when my stepdaughter is sick, all she wants is mom. Around 10 a.m., I received an excited phone call from Amy, "Ben is crawling!" It was the first time he crawled and I missed it.

Ever since he had learned to roll, I had spent at least 30 minutes a morning with Ben trying to help him crawl. I would lay him on the floor, place a light-up windup toy a few feet in front of him and cheer him on as he struggled to get to the toy. I saw him prop himself up into girlie pushup position for the first time. I saw him get on his knees for the first time. I saw him crawl backwards for the first time and worked with him for weeks on end trying to move forward (Most kids crawl backward first). I would help him get into the official crawling position when he struggled, hoping it would catch on. I did SO much work, yet I missed the big moment. I was furious.

The Overnight Family Man

Later that same day, Amy left Ben at The Buzz with me while she took her daughter to the doctor. Within 15 minutes of him being with me, as I carried him around The Buzz while I cleaned, he looked me in the eye and said, "Mama." This wasn't a mimicking moment like when he said "Daddy" on Christmas Day. This was legit! This was his first word! It was a monumental moment! And I witnessed it! And I was mad!

Everyone, and I mean EVERYONE, with children has sworn to me that every baby's first word is "Dadda" because it is the easiest word to say. Yet, my son said mama first. I am the one who spends all day with him. I am the one who cares for him the majority of the time. Why didn't he say "dadda" first?! To rub it in, he spent the next hour saying "mamma" over and over and over and OVER AND OVER AND OVER again.

The next day I had to work at The Buzz again; my stepdaughter was still sick. Around 10 a.m. I get a text from Amy. Apparently Ben decided to hit numerous major milestones that week. Her text informed me that Ben had sat up by himself for the first time. I actually screamed, "YOU HAVE GOT TO BE KIDDING ME!" (The customers were regulars, so when I explained my outburst they were fine with it.) I had missed another milestone! In the span of 24 hours, he learned to crawl, talk and sit. This was HUGE, yet I was upset. Yes, I know how selfish that was of me, but deal with it. At least I am being honest.

The day only got worse. Around 5 p.m. Amy stopped by The Buzz so we could go out to dinner. Her ex-in-laws were in town and watching the older kids, providing Amy and I with a chance to grab dinner with just one child in tow. On the way to the restaurant, my tire exploded. When I write exploded, I mean it EXPLODED! Thank God I was only driving about 15 mph around a bend, there were no kids in the car and Amy was behind me in her car (my jack is broken; without Amy's I was screwed).

So I changed the tire and turned into a hot, filthy, sweaty mess. Nothing … I repeat … NOTHING … is worse than changing a tire in Florida!

I then drive one block on my spare before … MY SPARE GOES FLAT!

I was sick to my stomach angry! I was ready to smash my car

to bits with my tire iron!

As I sat on the ground, stared at my flat spare and cursed my life, Amy sat next to me with Ben on her knee.

"Dadda!" I heard.

I looked to Ben. Amy looked to Ben. Amy and I then looked at each other and said almost in unison, "Did he just say…"

Before we could finish, as though it was a scene out of a cheesy Lifetime movie, Ben repeated on cue, "Dadda!"

That's my boy.

Thanks Little Dude. That made up for everything.

3-9-12
Facebook Update:

I have made the beds, fed the dogs, cleaned the bottles, dropped one kid off at school and fed and played with the baby before putting him down to nap. Now it is time to transcribe five hours of taped interviews for multiple articles. I'm a cross between Mrs. Brady and Mark Twain … you know you sweat me.

3-12-12
Facebook Update:

I remember when Spring Break was a break … now it is an extra kid hanging on me as I try to work.

3-16-12
A Letter to My Stepson to be Read in Two to Three Decades

Dear Stepson,

I am writing this on March 16, 2012, but I am having you read it many years later, probably when you are in your 20s or 30s, have children or a child of your own, and can fully respect what I am writing.

You were a good kid when you were 6, but you took everything your mom and I gave to you for granted. That didn't make you bad; it made you like every middle class suburban kid in America at the time and probably today. And, I am sure you did not get better with age. I did not fully appreciate anything my parents did for me at any time I lived under their roof, nor did any of my friends, and I am sure you were the same as a teen.

I am also sure that you and I butted heads quite a bit over the years and that while I can't think of any examples as I write this (because you are only 6 right now), I am positive you can rattle off quite a few off the top of your head. All fathers and sons go through their share of battles. Lord knows my father and I did. It is part of growing up. Teenage boys want independence, they want to be their own men, and rebelling against the man in the house, screaming at their fathers that they do not need them and that they are fine on their own, pulling away from the parental control they feel is holding them back, is completely normal.

What I fear made our relationship even more contentious is that while I love you like my blood son, you are not. I fear that teenage you always wondered if I truly love you as much as your younger brother and that this angst showed itself during our arguments. As I write this, I dread the day you disobey me and yell, "You're not my real dad!" I know that as you are reading this when you are in your 20s or 30s, you are smiling, knowing you said that stinging comment dozens of times.

What I hope is that you have since gotten over that fear and know that I love you like my own. But, just in case you do not, I want to remind you what I did on March 11, 2012.

You had been pestering me for weeks to help you start a garden. I have no idea what put that idea in your head, but it was all you wanted to do. When I realized how much it meant to you, I promised I would help. We had that giant screened in back patio at the home we rented (this was right before I sold my film for a billion dollars and we moved into the mansion you were raised in). I figured that patio would be a great place to grow your garden since it would allow you to tend to it whenever you wanted because it was safe for you to be out there on your own. Also, your spring vacation was coming up and I figured it would be a great way to keep you busy so I could work in peace.

There was just one issue – that back patio was a mess. It was covered in pollen, like a snow fall, and the recent rain storms had turned at least half of the pollen into a green sludge. That rental home was beautiful but also poorly made and the patio's drainage problem was at the top of the list. The pollen sludge had accumulated like a swamp at the back of the patio and become a mosquito haven. We had not had time to clean it during the pollen season – your brother's birth and the coffee shop opening took a lot of our time. So, we just avoided that porch like the plague until we could find time to clean it. Because we had not cleaned it, the spiders moved in, turning it into a scene out of the disturbing 1970s B-movie *Kingdom of Spiders* that I forced you to watch dozens of times as a teenager.

Getting the patio back in order was a tall undertaking, but I promised you I would do it and on March 11, 2012 I set out to make good on my promise.

There were just two small problems:

1. I had FOUR breaks in the same knuckle on my middle finger on my left hand, the result of a flag football play gone TERRIBLY wrong. This play, by the way, led to my retirement from the game. Heart breaking ... I know.

2. Our power washer was broken, which meant I had to scrub the patio using a garden hose and scrub brush on a broom handle.

These two small problems equaled one large problem – PAIN. It hurt buddy; my finger throbbed the entire time. The doctor ordered me to be light on the typing and to avoid the gym; he did not say anything about scrubbing a patio, but I am sure he would have frowned upon it if asked.

Halfway through the job – two hours in – I was ready to quit. I could not take another second of it. Each time I pressed the scrub brush against the patio and scraped the pollen off, it felt like my finger was re-breaking. It was terrible. But I didn't have the heart to disappoint you. I didn't have the heart to tell you that we could not start a garden during your week off from school because I could not properly clean the patio due to a finger break I incurred while playing flag football. There was no way I could have stomached the look of disappointment I am sure you would have had. And, to be honest, there was no way I could have handled you complaining all week that I disappointed you. But, most importantly, I loved you and wanted to do something special with you, such as growing that garden.

While I painfully cleaned that patio I realized that there were few people in the world I would have done that for and everyone else on that list was blood related to me. It reminded me that while you had a different last name than me, that I loved you like you were my blood son.

I hope that as you read this, you have a child of your own so you can appreciate that something as simple as cleaning a patio with a broken finger truly does show off what true love is. You are and always will be my son. There is nothing I would not do for you.

And Ben, if you are reading this and saying that I never did anything like that for you ... get over it dude. I gave you your good looks. What else do you want from me?

Love you,
Dad

3-22-12
Facebook Update:

I learned a valuable lesson today. If your 8-month-old who always needs attention suddenly leaves you alone for a long time, it is probably because he is rubbing vomit all over himself.

3-23-12
Do You Remember?

Dear Stepdaughter,

After I wrote a letter to your older brother last week, I realized you were the only member of the family to not have a letter written to you. I promise that you are not last because you are least, but rather because I have had the hardest time categorizing our relationship.

Your younger brother obviously looks at me as his father. Your older brother and I have a unique relationship because he has memories of his biological father, photographs in his mind to put to the voice on the other end of those phone conversations with him. Yet, I am the one who is raising him as a young boy. He often says he has two fathers – his "real father" and "the father who takes care of him."

But you ... you have no memories of your biological father. I often wonder if you are confused. There is this man on the other end of the phone saying he is your father, yet you call me daddy. What do you think a father is? You are too young to self-debate whether or not a father is the man who raises you or the man who conceived you. When you are capable of such rational thought, on what side of the argument will you be? And I often wonder if you have any memories of your life before I was part of it.

We met when you were just a little over a year old so it seems impossible that you can remember a life without me. But still ...I wonder.

Do you remember what life was like before you were a smart aleck? That is a trait I instilled in you. Your mom is not a smart aleck, nor is your older brother. I am. And I taught you everything I knew. I took you under my wing. I did so by trying to get under your skin 24/7, telling you that your pink shirt was really green, that your Dora the Explorer shirt was really an Olivia shirt, or that we were having rocks for dinner. When I first began bugging you, you didn't understand sarcasm and would flip out and angrily yell at me that I was wrong or lying. Your mom would get upset with me. She would lecture me that I shouldn't pick on a little kid so much. But as time wore on, you picked up on what I was doing and began dolling it back to me and using sarcasm to annoy the hell out of your older brother and mom, both whom do NOT understand sarcasm. Everyone calls your baby brother my mini-me because he looks just like me, but in a way you are also my mini-me because you have adopted so much of my personality.

Do you remember what life was like before you had this big mean bald guy telling you what to do? We butt heads a lot ... A LOT. You are constantly testing me, always grabbing junk food when I say no, running in the house faster after I tell you to stop running or refusing to go to bed, even when it is midnight and you are so tired your eyes look like they are ready to bleed. Do you remember what life was like before punishments included me throwing away your candy or putting your favorite toys in timeout for days and days? Do you remember what life was like before you had a father who knew how to scare you without raising his voice?

Do you remember what life was like before I would poke

your belly to make you laugh, even when you are in a terrible mood? Do you remember what life was like before I was there to catch you as you jumped into the pool? Do you remember what life was like before I was there to hug you after school, bathe you after dinner and carry you to bed at night? Do you remember what life was like before I was there to play tea party with you, toss you in the air and catch you, bounce you on my knee and sing the Lone Ranger song, sing your favorite songs with you and tell you how much I love you?

You have recently begun a relationship with your biological father. You still don't really know him, but you talk to him on the phone from time to time and when he calls. You call him your "new daddy" and, to be honest, it bothers me a bit. I get jealous. I know you have to establish a relationship with him and I know the "new daddy" tag does not mean I have been replaced; it is your way of saying that you have two dads. But it still bothers me. When I hear you saying that, I realize that I am not ready to share your love, even if it is with your "real" dad. You're my little girl. You're daddy's little girl and I am your daddy.

You didn't used to call me daddy. At first, you called me "Pepa" for some strange reason. And then, following your older brother's lead, you began calling me Paul. As you grew older and you knew me longer, Paul faded away and you began to call me daddy, which you still call me today. (Well, except when you are mad at me. Then you call me "Poopy Paul.")

I wonder if you remember what life was like before you called me daddy. And I wonder if the day will ever come in which you will cease to call me by that name.

Do you remember what your life was like before I was your dad?

I remember what life was like before you were my daughter. As frustrating as you can be, my memories of my life without you are dark. Life without you was lonely.

I love you,
Daddy ... aka Poopy Paul

3-29-12
Facebook Update:
I am staring at my son playing right now ... so full of energy

... so cute ... looking so much like me ... and all I can think is, "I HATE YOU! I HATE YOU! I HATE YOU! Why didn't you let me sleep for one second last night?!?!?! WHY?!?!?"

4-7-11
Facebook:

I had someone in Ybor yell out to my son yesterday, "Yo, that baby has a dope ass face!" Still not sure what to make of it.

4-13-12
Future Met?

I'm pretty honest with myself about my son's future as a professional athlete ... he has no future.

As much as I love playing and watching sports, I am not blind to the level of my athletic abilities. I am average. I am average height. I am average weight. I have an average build. I have average speed and average coordination.

In high school, I was the kid good enough to make the varsity soccer team but not good enough to stand out. There is nothing wrong with such a feat. It meant I was one of the best 16 players in the school, but not one of the best three or four. I was a good athlete, but not a stud athlete.

I hate these fathers who were average or even below average athletes when they were kids yet, in a completely serious tone, talk about how they expect their children to be star athletes one day. Huh? Do they not understand genetics? There is a reason why NBA players I grew up watching now have sons playing in the NBA while Johnny the Wing Eating Champ from the corner bar does not have any children in professional sports ... well, unless you count competitive eating as a sport.

However, I will push Ben to pursue some sort of athletic endeavors. Sports are important to the development of children for more reasons than I have room to list in this story, with the most important being that chicks dig athletes.

But, again, I do not expect Ben to be a great athlete. If he is, of course I'd be happy for him. If he is not – whatever. I will never be a parent who expects more out of his son that I should.

However ... it is tempting to think he could be a great

athlete.

Last week, Ben and I had our first catch. Seriously. We had a catch. I swear.

He was being extra needy last week. All he wanted to do was play with me and would not let me do one second of work. It is difficult to find ways to entertain an eight-month-old baby for hours in a way that is fun for me. There is only so long I can tickle him, toss him in the air, play peak-a-boo, sing to him or talk to him using a hand puppet before I begin to go completely nuts. (Yes, I have a hand puppet with which I talk to him, so what?! Oh, wait, you mean the fact that I use one means I am already nuts. Point well taken.) So I decided to try to teach him to play baseball. Yes, it seemed ridiculous to try to teach an eight-month old to play baseball, but it was opening day of Major League Baseball, so it also seemed appropriate.

I dressed him in his Mets uniform, put him on the floor a few feet from me, and tossed him a little yellow ball. It bounced off the ground and blasted him in the face. He cried like a baby for five minutes, and when he finished I tossed him the ball again ... and it again blasted him in the face and he again cried like a baby. (My son really needs to grow up and stop crying so much. He's eight months old for Christ's sake!)

My plan was not working, but I would not be deterred. I was determined. Plus, it was kind of funny to see my son getting hit in the face with a ball. (That's a joke people! Calm down!) So I tossed it lighter, bouncing it a foot from him so it rolled the last foot or two to him. I did it again and again for an hour, doing so in slow motion, hoping he would see my form and mimic it. And guess what? He did! He actually picked the ball up and threw it back to me! It only made it a few inches, but he did it! Once would have been a fluke. But he threw it to me over two dozen times. I thought, "My god! My son is a stud athlete!"

I videotaped it and put it on Facebook so the world could see. I sent the video via text message to all my friends. I called Amy and bragged that our son was going to play in the Major Leagues.

When Amy got home, Ben showed off his skills to her. I rolled him the ball and he threw it back to me. Again, the ball only flew a few inches in the air, but it was a throw nonetheless. Prior to seeing him throw, she laughed off my excitement. After seeing his athletic display, she too was fired up. What impressed Amy so much was that she noticed he was picking the ball up with his left hand and then placing it in his right hand to throw it. I immediately proclaimed, "He already knows he is right handed! He is a star athlete and a genius!"

No matter what I tell myself, no matter how honest I try to be, I guess there will always be a part of me that hopes my son is a star athlete. I guess that is part of being a man. We all want our sons to be studs.

Unfortunately, my son has my genetics. The next day, I rolled him the ball. He threw it to me. I rolled it to him again, and he picked a piece of fuzz from the carpet, ate it and gagged. He then crawled away from the ball as though he had no idea what it was.

Chances are, my son peaked at eight months old. Or perhaps he will be an athletic stud. You never know. Regardless, I love him.

Of course, if he is not a great athlete, that does not mean he can't be a stud. He also got my looks! Go ahead and laugh, but have you seen how hot Amy is? Trust me, my personality is not THAT good.

4-14-12
Facebook Update:
I think every montage in Rocky IV is pure gold. Yes, I am watching Rocky IV on a Saturday night and posting about it on Facebook. I'd say this is parenthood but I would have done this single too. God bless you Rocky for ending the Cold War. Yes, we can all change.

4-14-12
Facebook Update:
Left my longtime gym – Leo's Beach Park Gym – today. Been working out there since 1999. I'll miss the place. I was friends with all the members. But I needed a place with a daycare now that I am with Ben so much, so I joined the Y.

4-25-12
Facebook Update:

I taught my stepson everything I know about fishing today ... which means I taught him that he needs a fishing pole.

4-27-12
Trapped Under a Baby!
Tuesday, April 17, 2012
10:15 a.m.

He was finally asleep. Ben had a strong nine-month run of good health but one week in the Y's daycare system took care of that. He had been crying for one straight hour, refusing to sleep, his head burning up with a fever and his stomach churning with a bug. But he had finally fallen asleep. I don't know if it was my hand lovingly patting his butt or the soft chorus of the *Charles In Charge*'s theme song that I was singing into his ear, nor did I care. He was asleep!

As I always do when I get him to finally accept his visit from the Sand Man, I gently carried him to his crib and laid him down. He usually does not stir. On that day, however, he immediately woke and began crying again, so I quickly scooped him back up and began patting and singing again, "A new boy in the neighborhood, he lives down stairs and it's understood ..."

10:20 a.m.

He was finally back asleep. I took him to the crib. He woke again. Damn it! "... he's there just to take good care of me, like he's one of the family..."

10:25 a.m.

Asleep ... crib ... awake ... "Charles In Charge of our days and our nights..."

10:30 a.m.

It was not working. He was not letting me put him down. He was sick and needy and wanted the comfort of daddy. So I sat down on my bed, lay slightly back, patted his butt and sung him back to sleep, opting for *The Facts Of Life* theme song.

11:00 a.m.

He had been asleep for 30 minutes so I again tried to stand up, hoping to get him to his crib. I had a lot of work to do. I had deadlines to meet. But as soon as I moved an inch, he began to wake. Damn it, I thought. Luckily, I had my phone next to me and I texted my client, explaining that my son was sick. She is a mother herself so I knew she would understand. Ben needed his sleep and if the only way he was going to get it was on my chest and by me sitting still, then so be it. He needed to get healthy.

11:15 a.m.

My god I was bored! I am a father of three! I have a fulltime writing career plus help with the coffeehouse when I can. I cannot remember the last time I sat around for 45 minutes doing nothing. It sounds relaxing in theory, but in practice it was BORING. I was not used to it and was going stir crazy. As I looked at his adorable face with his rosy red sick cheeks, however, my boredom-induced anger was flushed away. He was worth it, I thought.

11:30 a.m.

The only thing that had kept me sane for the past 75 minutes had been my cellphone. I surfed the net, sent some text messages and played on Facebook, but I had officially run out of things to do. I don't have any games on my cell phone. I decided to risk it and turn on the TV. If I kept the sound low enough, I rationalized, he would not wake up. There was one problem, however – the remote control was on the far side of the room and I could not move to get it without waking Ben! I had no television to help pass the time! Perhaps I could have gotten up, grabbed the remote and sung him back to sleep, but what if I could not get him to close his eyes again and the lack of sleep impeded his healing process? As I looked at Ben cuddled up on my chest, I realized it was all worth it to stay still and not risk waking him. He was so damn cute.

11:45 a.m.

My cell phone battery was ready to die. Considering it was my only source of entertainment, watching the battery's juice slowly dwindle over the past 90 minutes was like watching an oxygen meter showing a room losing oxygen during a cave-in. I figured the phone had enough power for a handful of text messages, though, so I shot Amy a text explaining the situation, hoping she would have some advice on how to slowly get up and put him in his crib without waking him. All she texted back was, "You're a good dad." That's it?!?! After three kids that is all she could write? She didn't have ANY advice? Even worse, that text was all my phone had left in it. It died. I was without a phone. I officially had nothing to do but stare at the wall! But when I looked at Ben's angelic face drooling on my shirt, I realized he was worth it.

12:15 p.m.

I had to pee. I had to pee REAL badly. I had chugged a large latte right before Ben had fallen asleep, so not only could I not nap to pass the time, but my bladder was crying out for the toilet. I tried to move but he began to stir! OH MY GOD! I thought. If I moved he would wake and if he woke he would not fall back asleep and if he did not fall back asleep he would not get better and if he did not get better because I was not strong enough to hold in my pee, I would be a jerk and a bad dad! I was in pain! But when I looked at his peaceful face, I realized … I realized he was an ugly, big headed, snot nosed jerk! I was so mad at him at that moment! WAKE UP! I thought to myself. FOR THE LOVE OF GOD WAKE UP!

12:30 p.m.

It had officially gotten out of hand. He usually only naps for 60 – 90 minutes. He was at 135 minutes and showed no signs of waking. I was bored. I had no phone. I could not sleep. I had to pee. And I was getting hungry! But I dared not move. By that point it was more than letting him sleep, it was a test of will! It was like watching a bad movie to the end even though it was painful to do so. After logging so much time, you feel like you at least have to see it through to the end. That was how I felt about Ben's nap. To wake him at that point would have meant I had suffered in vain.

1:30 p.m.

I was losing it. I was REALLY losing it. And then … HE FINALLY WOKE UP!

Usually when Ben wakes from a nap it is the cutest moment of my day. He opens his eyes, smiles at me, giggles and says, "Dadda! Dadda! Dadda!" On that day, he opened his eyes, grimaced, moaned and exploded. Parents call it a blowout. It is when a baby poops so violently that it shoots out their diaper and up their back. Ben's blowout made it all the way to his hair. It was gross. I was smelly. It was everywhere. And it was a fantastic sight to behold! The bellyache that caused it had woken him! He was awake!

I rushed him to the bathroom, stripped him naked, wiped his butt and back, tossed him into the tub, peed the greatest pee in the history of mankind, turned on the bathtub, scrubbed him, dressed him, made a quick sandwich for myself and a bottle for him, loaded him into my car and left to pick my stepson up from school.

On the way there, he fell back asleep.

Jerk.

5-4-12
My Little Piggybank

As I write this, my eyes have never been heavier in my entire life.

I have never been this tired.

I am more tired than I was during triple session soccer practices in high school.

I am more tired than I was following weeklong parties in college ... err ... study sessions in college.

I am more tired that I was when I arrived in Tampa in 1999 after a 20 hour drive.

I am more tired than I have ever been on a movie set, and those work days are usually 20 hours long for a week straight.

It turned out that being stuck under a sleeping sick baby was just the start of a long week. Ben could not kick that illness.

Five different doctors in seven days could not solve it.

Countless thermometers crammed into his butt could not scare it out of him.

A chest x-ray was inconclusive.

Stomach settling medication did not stop his cries.

Children's Advil and Tylenol combined could not bring his fever down for long.

Prescribed antibiotics could not destroy the enemy within him.

Even a catheter did nothing but increase the volume of his screams.

It was frustrating. I wanted to grab a doctor by the shirt, throw him against the wall and demand that he make my baby well! For the love of God, I wanted to yell, you get paid to cure illness yet not one of five of you can make my baby's pain go away! DO SOMETHING! I wanted to scream.

Our first doctor visit was to an after hour pediatric clinic. Doctor #1 looked at Ben's throat and ears. He listened to his chest.

And he looked in his nose. He found nothing wrong. His diagnosis was that Ben had a virus and it would run its course by morning.

When he still had a fever of 102.3 two days later, Amy took him to his regular pediatrician and he was tested for strep, from which his older brother was suffering. The throat culture turned up negative so Doctor #2 said it was just a virus and would run its course.

The next night he screamed in pain for THREE straight hours, howling like he was digesting glass. I rushed him to the emergency room and he was diagnosed with a stomach bug by Doctor #3. It will run its course, she said.

It did not. The next day his fever spiked at 102.5. If it was running its course, the fever should have been going down, not up. I took him back to the afterhours clinic where a new doctor, Doctor #4, performed a chest x-ray and told me it was probably bronchiolitis, a common illness in babies. He prescribed antibiotics and said that it would ... yes ... RUN ITS COURSE! The only reason I did not kill the doctor when he sputtered those words was because I was still laughing my butt off following the chest x-ray. If you have never seen a baby receive one, they place him, standing up, inside a plastic tube that completely encases him when they perform the x-ray. I should have felt terrible for Ben as he cried in fear, but I instead laughed. He looked like one of those action figures you see stuff inside a plastic case. I know ... I'm mean.

The next day his fever went even higher! I rushed him to a different ER where he was checked by Doctor #5 for a urinary tract infection. They do so by thrusting a catheter into his penis and drawing urine from it. It bled. His penis bled! He cried louder than I have ever heard a baby cry and I wanted to cry for him. HIS PENIS WAS BLEEDING! And when all tests came back negative ... well ... you know what Doctor #5 told me.

The whole experience was simply exhausting.

Ben did not sleep more than an hour straight throughout the entire ordeal. And the doctor's trips are excruciating. Not only was he crying in pain and/or fear, but he was also fussy. He wanted to crawl around and explore, not be held for two to three hours straight. But it is a doctor's office, home to every virus on the planet. I wanted him to get better, not sicker. I know they sterilize an ER and doctor's office, but it still sits in the back of my mind that dozens of snotty nosed kids a day touch everything. Ben squirmed the ENTIRE time. By the time I left each visit, I was mentally and physically worn down.

When his fever still did not break the day after the second ER trip, I was ready to cry. I wanted Ben to be healthy and, as selfish as it sounds, I wanted sleep and a day free of 24 hour crying.

Then, that night, the source of all his pain was discovered ... by Amy ... in his diaper.

He pooped a dime.

Yes, you read that correctly. Ben pooped a dime. He had found a dime, swallowed it, digested it and sat in pain for an entire week as it made its way through his body. The 10-cent intruder caused his fever that was not going to break until he forced it from his body. We are not sure where he found the dime. Our home is pretty secure. My guess is he scooped it up in a pile of sand he was shoveling into his mouth at the beach. Yes, my son eats dimes, sand and basically anything else you put in front of him. We try to pull everything out of his mouth, but I guess one of us looked away for a split second at the beach and were not able to stop the pile of sand from entering his gullet.

When his fever finally broke and he was healthy, part of me felt terrible for him, contemplating the pain with which he must have been dealing.

Part of me was scared. What if he had choked on the dime and died or if it had punctured something internally and killed him? What if he swallowed a quarter? What if there was MORE money in him?

And part of me looked at him and thought, You idiot. You swallowed a dime!

Seriously, my son is an idiot.

And thus, the name of Ben "Piggybank" Guzzo was thrust upon him by Amy and me. No matter what he does from here on out, even if he cures cancer on the same night that he breaks the homerun record, he will be forever known in our household as Piggybank.

5-8-12
Facebook Update:

House is so quiet. Amy at meeting, Ben asleep and the other two kids are scared of me. Time to crack a beer.

5-11-12
Facebook Update
I went to my first school recital tonight ... O ... M ... G... how the F did my parents make it through so many of those?! I saw maybe five parents having an honest good time, and I am pretty sure by the glazed look in their eyes they were stoned out of their minds.

5-22-12
Facebook Update:
I just realized that this week is the fourth anniversary of my friend Ben's death. Still miss the hell out of him. Named my son after him.

5-25-12
A letter to my son's namesake
It is hard to believe that it has been four years since we last spoke. A lot has happened since then.

I grew sideburn chops and actually kept them for a year before I shaved. I bought a new used car FINALLY. (The Grand Am needed to be retired.) I tried a few new restaurants. I saw a blimp. Oh yeah, I also got engaged to a woman and moved in with her after dating her for less than six months. Did I mention that she has two kids? Oh, before I forget, we were engaged for a whole three or four weeks before she got pregnant. A few months after that, she opened a coffeehouse.

I've long thought you would have appreciated the twists and turns my life has taken over the past two years more than anyone. You always did respect the way I would make life's decisions on a whim, how I always lived on gut instinct rather than analyzing everything for hours before I acted. When I temporarily left college when I was 19, you were the only person who didn't lecture me on how stupid I was acting. Instead, all you said was, "You'll go back if you want to and won't if you don't." When I decided to move to Tampa without a job or any knowledge of the city, you didn't pepper me with questions on why I was making such a move. Instead, you said, "I'll get you a pink flamingo." And I'll never forget how disappointed you were when you could not find one.

Of all my friends, I always thought you understood me the best, which was odd considering we were polar opposites. You analyzed everything a million times over and cared about the minutia of life.

I have also long thought you would have been the most supportive of my new family. None of the old crew from New Jersey has come to Tampa to meet my new family. I don't think that makes them bad people. I'm just as guilty as they are. There is plenty of our old crew I have not seen since they started a family. It's hard. I have three kids, my own career and a fiancée with a business to run. And most of them have a similar list of responsibilities.

However, you are the one member of our old crew who I know would never have used anything as an excuse for not visiting me. You would have been in Tampa with your wife and son just a few weeks after I got engaged and would have been here days after my son was born. That was what made you so special. You were the most selfless of our entire crew. And you respected friendship more than anyone I have ever known. Friends were always more than friends to you. Friends were family.

I talk about you a lot. You are part of all my stories – the days we spent hacky sacking in front of the student center like hippies without a care in the world, the bar we built in your apartment, our cross country trip to see the Grand Canyon, and, of course, our weekend-long trips to Bryn Mawr College, the all-girls college for the super-rich. We got drunk with a princess and the daughter of the inventor of the CD at that college!

I also lament that I did not have one more weekend with you. Four years ago, I was in LA with my brother for business and we decided to go home a day early. As we were packing, you called me to tell me you were in LA for business too. I could have stayed one more night; I had not yet changed my flight. But I decided to go home anyway. I told you we would catch up that summer.

I never saw you again.

A few months later, you took your own life.

I won't be one of those clichéd guys who writes that I was angry with you for killing yourself and leaving a wife and son

The Overnight Family Man

behind. I hate when people say BS like that. If I was angry, that would mean I thought you were thinking rationally when you did it and that you selfishly wanted them to suffer. I have to believe that you were mentally dead at that point; that the man I once knew had ceased to be, eaten away by the depression I have since learned had plagued you since childhood.

The world has gone on without you. Your wife is engaged and recently birthed a gorgeous son with her soon-to-be husband. Your son has grown into a fine boy, handsome and well-behaved. You would be proud of him. But, he has a new dad now and, considering how young he was when you left him, I am sure he has very little firsthand memory of you. I am sure he only knows you from photos and stories.

Your memory continues to haunt me, though.

Not a week goes by in which I don't think of you. That is not lip service. I often wonder what both our lives would be like if things had turned out differently. I picture you coming to Tampa once a year. Your children would play with my children until they all fell asleep in sleeping bags as part of a sleepover. You, your wife, Amy and I would then stay up late into the night, drinking, reminiscing, laughing and talking about how odd it is that we are both family men considering the immature college kids we once were. Back then, it was hard to imagine ourselves as responsible adults.

And I wonder, in this alternate universe, what would my son's name be?

I miss you man. I miss you so much.

This sucks.

You were supposed to be here with me. You were supposed to have met my son. My son is not supposed to have your name.

6-1-12
Can We Have One Nice Night Out?!

It's hard to have a social life with three kids.

None of our single friends want to invite us to anything. One kid is kryptonite to a single person's party or event. A family with three kids is ... well ... what's worse than kryptonite? A bag of flaming poop?

Not even our friends with kids want to invite us to their

parties. Any kid-friendly party is going to be overrun with kids. When you start inviting families with three or more kids, the event goes from overrun to ... well ... a bag of flaming poop. In fact, not even our friends with three kids want us at their parties for the same reason. It's family on family crime!

The list of civic events we are invited to is short. With three kids to look after, we often have to shuck our civic responsibilities. So, when guest lists are made for important events, our names rarely make the cut.

When our names do make the cut, it then becomes tough to find a babysitter. It is hard enough to find a babysitter we trust with our kids. It is even harder to find one we trust who wants the overwhelming responsibility to look after three kids.

And even when we can find a sitter, the cost of a ticket to the event may be too great. I am not sure if anyone with three kids can ever claim to be on anything but a tight budget. Even billionaires must have a problem keeping up with the financial responsibly of three children – they don't just have to buy one Porsche, but three.

Then last week, everything fell into line for Amy and me.

I recently completed a book on the history of Tampa's India community, *From Indian to Indian-Americans: How Tampa Bay's Indian Community Was Built*. To thank me for the book, the Indo-U.S. Chamber of Commerce provided Amy and me with tickets to their annual black tie affair, The Banyan Ball. At first it seemed like we would not be able to attend as our babysitter was not available until 8 p.m. and the event began at 6:30. It seemed like it was going to be yet another in a long line of social failures due to having three children. Then, Amy's ex-laws came to town and agreed to babysit the children until the sitter was available.

It was an amazing feeling! Amy and I not only had a rare opportunity to go out without the kids in tow, but we got to dress to the nines and could brag that we were attending THE event in the city that night, an event with a guest list filled with a who is who of the Tampa Bay community, both Indians and non-Indians. And we did not have to break our piggy banks (not Ben) to go or feel guilty about spending money we could have spent on the kids (always an issue). Again, everything was falling into place ... or so we thought. Once everything seemed to be set, everything then proceeded to go wrong.

First, Ben got sick. It was just the croup, a common virus that babies catch that has more bark than bite. It brings only a slight fever to the baby, but a nasty seal-like cough that shakes the walls. Amy and I both debated whether we could leave Ben with a sitter. While there was no danger of the illness getting worse, the cough makes it hard for the baby to sleep. We both pictured Ben waking throughout the evening and crying for us to comfort him, only to find us not home. It was heartbreaking to imagine, but we decided we needed to go out. Again, our opportunities to go to events as high-end as the Banyan Ball are few. We couldn't pass it up because of a cough.

Just when it seemed like we were in the clear, Amy threw out her hips. Apparently, Ben's big head had done some major damage to her on its way out. She ignored the pain for 10 months but last week it become too great to handle. Unable to stand up straight, she had to walk hunched over, one hand on her hip to brace herself, and her butt sticking straight out – the only posture that seemed to alleviate the pain. She was walking like an old woman with hemorrhoids.

Then, my tooth came out. I have a long history of problems with my dental crowns. Ever since I had my front teeth crowned following a 1997 mugging in New Jersey that saw my mouth shattered, I seem to be in a dentist chair at least once a month to have one cemented back in. Usually, it is not a big deal. My dentist usually can put it back in the day it comes loose or the following morning at the latest. With the Banyan Ball on the horizon, the crown fell out on 5:01 on Friday night, one minute after my dentist's office closed for the entire weekend! Worse yet, it was my front tooth! The event was on Saturday. There was no way to have it repaired!

We finally had the opportunity to attend a great event, and we looked like a redneck and an old woman with butt problems. Fantastic!

For most couples, such catastrophes would have kept them home. But when you have three kids, a sitter and free tickets to a high end affair, nothing … I MEAN NOTHING … can keep you from it. I crammed my tooth into my mouth with denture cream and Amy slipped into a sexy dress, uncomfortable heals and stood up straight as an arrow, grinding her teeth in pain. We kissed our coughing baby good night and booked out the door before anything else bad could happen ... and, of course, something else did.

I wore the wrong suit.

Seriously.

It was a black tie affair, which means a black suit. I somehow put on a blue suit without realizing it. I am that dumb. And we did not realize it until we got to the event. Not sure if a blue suit was allowed, we raced back home and I changed while Amy swallowed an entire bottle of Ibuprofen. We then left before something else could go wrong ... and, of course, something else did.

I left the denture cream in the original suit. If my crown came out at the Banyan Ball, I had no way to put it back in. I did not realize that I had forgotten it until we re-arrived at the ball. It was already 7:30 p.m. at that point. The cocktail hour was over and dinner was ready to begin. To return home or even go to the store for a new tube would have made us way too late. Most couples may have skipped the ball at that point, but not couples with three kids. If my tooth came out, I would just have to be remembered as the redneck at the Banyan Ball.

Finally, however, karma was kind to us. My tooth never came out. Amy's hips stayed in place. The sitter never called to say Ben was waking up and miserable because of his cough. We actually were able to have a great date. We made new friends and bumped into old ones. We enjoyed some drinks. We ate a delicious dinner. My book even received two mentions in speeches by Indo-U.S. Chamber board members.

We had fun.

And in the morning, we were woken by three kids screaming they were hungry, thirsty, bored, etc.

Whatever.

We finally had one night.

6-7-12

Facebook Update:

I would once again like to tell everyone with parents around to help with the kids how much I hate them. Seriously ... not a joke. I have hatred in my heart for you. Please block me from seeing your updates on how nice a night or weekend you had because your parents watched your kids. I'm tired. And I hate.

6-8-12
Ben's BIG Discovery

Apparently, Ben is not happy hitting just one milestone in a day. Recently, for the second time in his short life, he hit three milestones in one day. It began early morning, May 28. Ben would not sleep all night. All he wanted to do was lie in our bed. No, correction, all he wanted was to crawl around our bed, forcing us to grab him time and time again before he fell off the edge. Each time one of us grabbed him, he would respond by punching us in the face – not slapping, but punching ... and doing so hard. The little dude packs quite a punch.

Finally deciding to give up on sleep, hours before the sun was set to rise, Amy began pressing him to perform some of the new "tricks" for the first time that she had been trying to teach him. Yes, we call them tricks, like he is a dog, but considering he walks on all fours, poops whenever he wants and eats anything off the ground, it's not that far of a stretch.

The trick she'd been pushing on him the hardest involved him holding a phone up to his ear and saying "Hello," which is especially hard considering it includes memory (remembering to hold the phone), coordination (holding the phone) and speaking (speaking). And on that morning, he did it ... he did it flawlessly. His "Hello" was the clearest word he had ever spoken, which was a milestone. Sure, babbling "mama" and "dadda" counts as his first words, but this was a well-articulated word ... well, as well-articulated as a baby can sound. It was a true milestone. But this ... this was not his finest moment that epic day.

Later that afternoon, he hit milestone number two. I have been working on his walking for two months. Each day when I picked up his older brother from school, I arrived 30 minutes early and had Ben walk around the playground with a baby walker that helps teach babies to walk. It's really no different than a walker a disabled adult would use, except that it is made of plastic, painted lime green and is a lot shorter. In the beginning, he was out of control. He would stumble a few feet, the walker would fly out in front of him and he would face plant onto the concrete. The problem was he was moving his upper body faster than his lower body; his balance was off, which is the hardest lesson for a baby to learn. But as the weeks went on, he got it. Using the walker, he would stroll from one side of the playground to the other, at least 25 yards in each direction, with the greatest of ease. Every parent waiting to pick up their child noticed his improvement and began mentioning that it would be any day before he was walking. A month later, they were still saying that. No matter how many times I tried to get Ben to walk on his own, he refused to do so. He would not even try, simply plopping onto his butt instead.

On that magical Monday, however, Amy placed him in the middle of the living room and asked him to walk to her. And he did … well, kind of. A first step is not what most people think. He did not turn into Carl Lewis overnight. He shuffled one foot forward and then dragged the next foot a few inches before falling face first. It was clumsy and un-poetic, but it was a first step nonetheless. It was a true monumental moment in his life. BUT, it was not THE milestone that grand day.

It happened that evening. Ben had been battling a nasty butt rash for days so whenever we could we would let him crawl around naked to let it air out. (Parenting is so glamorous!) Up to that point, the only news coming out of "naked baby crawling around the house" was a few loose turds hitting the floor. On this night, however, it happened. It finally happened. He found his penis!

Amy and I had been discussing Ben's disinterest in his penis for months. From what I understand, most baby boys grab it the moment it is exposed to the fresh air. But Ben never did. Not when we changed his diaper. Not when he was in the bath. Never. Then on that fairy tale of a day, he sat in the middle of the living room and discovered it. He played with it. He picked at it. He inspected it. He tugged on it. He moved it around. And then, he wouldn't let go of it and it became creepy. So I put his diaper back on. It was either that or pronounce Ben and his penis "Man and Wife."

Nonetheless, in the great annals of his life, this will be one of his greatest moments. Men are not led by their minds, which is why speaking was not as important. Nor are they led by their physical prowess, which is why walking was not as important. Men are led

The Overnight Family Man

around life by their penises. Everything they do is for the glory of that little ... err ... BIG organ. It was a monumental day for Ben. It was the day he began his long journey into slavery ... err ... manhood.

(Ben, if you are reading this, you probably want to kill me for writing this. Sorry dude. Please, please, please don't let this story be the reason you toss me in a state run home when I get old.)

6-24-12
Facebook Update:

I know the parents who think their kids do no wrong are offended when I say this, but it is true - my son Ben is a total jerk. He spends half the day knowingly trying to bother people. Yes, at 11 months old he knows how to bother people. He is a total jerk.

6-27-12
Facebook Update

I had one of those mornings with Ben in which I want to go back in time to November 2010 and cut my balls off.

6-28-12
Facebook Update

Why kjfjhefuwejfwemfkwo does kj fkjef fsekjf Ben feel the jkesfjeifueiei need to jkfksejfjkfh bang on my keyboard jkjfksfhiwej when I try to 2o849284nci23cxo3rifekje type?!?!?!

6-29-12
My Son Is A Jerk!

"Dude, stop," I said to Ben, trying – the key word being TRYING – to patiently scold him.

He was not listening. No, rather he listened to what I said but chose to ignore my request. He grabbed another Cheerio off his highchair's tray and dropped it to the ground, staring at me with a stone-faced look of disobedience.

I finally lost my cool.

"STOP!" I screamed , kneeling down to pick up the pile of Cheerios on the ground.

He then broke down in faux tears, pretending to be upset by

my scolding. I knew it was all an act, so I turned away from him, not wanting to give him any attention for his behavior. And when I did – SLAM SLAM SLAM! He wacked his tray three times in defiance with both hands, sending the remaining Cheerios flying to the ground. I stared at him in total awe. This is regular morning routine for us, yet it shocks me every time. My son is a jerk.

Yes, I just wrote that. My son is a jerk! He is only 11 months old and he is a total jerk! He is only 11 months old, but he goes out of his way to get under my skin. He is just 11 months old, but he already knows how to lie.

My days with Ben are becoming increasingly difficult due to his propensity for being a jerk. If I put him in his high chair, he screams bloody murder until I take him out; I cannot write when a baby is yelling in such a manner. But when I put him on the ground, he gets into everything.

If I place him in the living room, he picks up every one of his toys and tosses it over whatever I am using to barricade him in. For the next 20 minutes, all I hear is CRASH, CRASH, CRASH as his toys slam against the hardwood floor. The worst thing I ever did was teach him to throw at such a young age.

When he is out of toys to throw, he begins looking for ways to escape the living room. If it wasn't so annoying, it would be amazing to watch. He will push the plastic bin in which we keep his toys to the edge of the living room, in front of whatever I am using to keep him in, climb onto the bin and try to make his way to freedom. The problem is he cannot climb down, so I spend the morning rushing to him before he falls from the crate. Again, I get no work done.

His climbing goes beyond escape. I left a box sitting next to a hutch in our hallway. He climbed the box and grabbed everything from the top of the hutch and tossed it to the floor.

If I place him on the kitchen floor, he opens every drawer and cabinet he can reach and empties its contents. He never just places an item on the floor, either. He always has to throw it. And when he finds one that is especially loud – like a frying pan – he throws it over and over and over again. I cannot work with all that noise!

Yes, we need to child lock the drawers. We have done the

drawers and cabinets with dangerous items, but not the ones with Tupperware and other such things. That is not the point, though. The point is that Ben does these things to get under my skin! I see it in his eyes. Every time I tell him to stop, he shoots me that same cold disobedient stare, slowly grabs the next item he wants to toss while never taking his eyes off me, and then smashes it onto the floor. And then, he smiles at me. I swear he smiles at me; it is a sadistic smile too, like he is Baby Stewie from *Family Guy*.

Compounding my frustration is that no one believes me! Whenever I tell people that Ben is a jerk, they look at me like I am the jerk! Babies don't do things to get under your skin, they tell me. You're being ridiculous, they lecture me.

Even Amy thought I was crazy ... until this past weekend.

My three-year-old had been spending all day Friday screaming at Ben in the car, yelling at him to stop touching her and grabbing her. She is quite the terror, so we immediately believed that she was just in a bad mood and taking it out on poor Baby Ben. So on Saturday we switched her seat with that of my usually levelheaded six-year-old so that he was sitting next to Ben. Moments later, our six-year-old was screaming at Ben for the same reasons.

Curious, Amy slyly looked into her rearview mirror to see what was going on. It turned out, the older kids were right – Ben was bugging them. He was pinching the 6-year-old, grabbing his hands, kicking his seat, throwing whatever he could get his hands on at him and poking him. And he was doing it with that stare I have grown to know. As our 6-year-old got more and more frustrated, Ben's assault increased, with that disobedient smile on his face the whole time. Amy lost it.

"Ben's messing with him!" she whispered to me. "He is actually trying to bug him."

As our 6-year-old tried to pry Ben's hands off his bracelet, Ben's smile grew larger when he saw the bracelet begin to bend as though it was going to snap.

"Look at him," Amy whispered. "He really is a total jerk."

"I told you so!" I gleefully exclaimed, happy to finally be vindicated.

"I guess it shouldn't shock me," Amy laughed. "He is your son."

7-17-12
Facebook Update:
Stepson: Does anyone have red eyes?
Me: The devil.
Stepson: Who is the devil? Is he a Star Wars guy?
Me: No. He's from the Bible.
Stepson: Is that like Star Wars?
Me: Yes.

7-18-12
Facebook Update:
In the last year, I have called him a jerk, annoying, a bastard, obnoxious, disgusting, smelly, stinky, rank, stupid and more ... and, well, I meant it all. BUT, he is still the second best thing I ever helped to create (that Marion Cobretti Mix Tape I made with Gene Siudut in 1997 still tops the list).

Happy Birthday Little Dude. 17 more years and you're out of the house!

Love you.

7/20/12
Happy Birthday Ben ... Now Get The Heck Out!
Dear Ben,
Happy Birthday! As I pen this week's story, it is a few days before your first birthday – July 18, 2012. This is supposed to be the story in which I take a sentimental look back at the last year and discuss how fast it went, how quickly you are growing up and how much your birth meant to me. Instead, I am celebrating the fact that your mom and I kicked you out of our room!
Why would I celebrate tossing my own son from my room a few days before his birthday? Because, you were the worst roommate I ever had! And I lived with some pretty bad people:

- My college roommate was crazy – actually CRAZY. He once chased crows in the backyard at 2 in the morning. There were

NO crows out there. He was chasing figments of his imagination.

- My roommate when I lived in Ybor City used to forget to flush the toilet. On one occasion I came down with food poisoning and had to run to the bathroom for a good heave. When I thrust my face into the bowl, I was met with his digested dinner!

Ben, it may be hard to believe, but you were worse than the crazy guy and the toilet guy.

When you were born, because you were … uhh … unplanned … yeah, that's the word – unplanned … we did not have a bedroom for you. We were living in a two bedroom house. Your mom and I had one room and your brother and sister were still young enough that they could share a room. We could not put you in their room – a baby with two hyper little kids would not have worked. The only other room in the house that could have been used as a bedroom for you was the house's finished office, which we turned into a toy room. We discussed making that your room, but that room offered us sanctuary from your siblings. Whenever they grew overly-hyper, we banished them to the toy room and enjoyed a few moments of peace. If we gave that room to you, we would go nuts without it, we figured. So we put your crib in our bedroom.

Guess what Ben? By the time you turned one, you were so obnoxious that we were willing to lose that sanctuary on a part time basis. We moved your crib into the toy room. When you were sleeping, it became off limits to your brother and sister. We preferred to deal with your siblings' hyper behavior than share a room with you any longer.

You weren't bad as in you were using the bedroom to cut up cocaine you were selling on the streets to fund an international terror cell. You were just … well … you were just, as I have stated a few times already, a jerk.

Ben, there were afternoons that you napped in which I power washed our backyard's screened in porch that was connected to our bedroom and you didn't wake up. Yet, if I took one step inside the room you did. How is that even possible? A power washer didn't wake you but a creek in the floor did! Because of your odd sleeping behavior, your mom and I became prisoners in our own bedroom. We had to tiptoe around our own bedroom! Relaxing nights lying in bed and watching television were never relaxing. We were balls of stress throughout every second of programming we viewed, hoping that the volume wouldn't suddenly spike, praying that there were no loud explosions or gunshots that would shake you from your sleep, begging the TV gods to banish all those locally produced commercials that feature loudmouthed spokesmen screaming about deals at the top of their lungs, and keeping the volume so low on nights when you were obviously going to be a light sleeper that we needed to turn the hearing impaired subtitles on! As for conversations in our bedroom? Impossible! If you heard our voices you immediately jumped out of sand land.

Then there was the smell. Yes Ben, you stunk. No matter how well we bathed you and lotioned you, you wreaked. It's not your fault – you inherited that from your mother. Adding to the smell was your urine. We could smell a wet diaper on you from across the house. It always smelled like you ate a ton of asparagus yet we never once fed you one bite of the urine-tainting vegetable. And of course, not helping the situation was your delightful habit of tossing bottles across the room as we slept so that unbeknownst to us they would roll under furniture and rot.

Finally, your being in our room was beginning to affect your mom and my ... uh ... personal time. It was one thing for us to ... uhh ... express our love with you in the room when you were an infant. You would usually sleep through it (insert "because I am like a power washer" joke here) and if you woke you couldn't see over the crib anyway. But as you grew older, you could peer over the crib. There is NOTHING – I mean NOTHING – creepier than realizing one of your kids is watching you. (Well, maybe reading about your parents expressing their love is creepier.) That was the breaking point in our relationship as roommates. It was time for you to go.

However, despite all the reasons to toss you from my room, my first reaction to the decision was actually sadness (I do have a heart ... sometimes). Part of me loved you being there. Part of me loved knowing you were sleeping just inches from me. Part of me loved watching you sleep. Part of me loved turning toward your crib

The Overnight Family Man

in the morning and seeing you standing up and smiling at me, as though you had been waiting an hour for me to wake up and seeing my eyes open was the greatest thing to ever happen to you. Part of me … apparently a very small part of me.

As we placed you in your crib on your first night in your own room, my eyes began to well up with tears. You began to scream. They were just baby screams, the type of nonsensical howls that all babies make when they are upset. Yet, on that night, I felt like I could translate your screams. "Why are you leaving me daddy?" I heard. "Why don't you love me anymore? What did I do wrong?" It was awful.

Then, as we shut the door to your new room, I peered into my bedroom and saw your crib missing and thought, "HE IS GONE! HELL YEAH! I HAVE MY ROOM BACK!" Your mom and I sat in bed, watched TV and had a conversation without worrying about waking a baby. It was great.

I love ya Little Dude. You're my boy. But good riddance!

Happy first birthday Ben! You are the best thing I ever helped to make – even better than that 80s mix tape I made for my college girlfriend, and that tape had Run DMC on it!

8/10/12
Saying Good Bye to Habit

The small red throw rug she slept on most of the day is gone. As is the cage filled with blankets and pillows she used to escape our other dog Duke when his hyper activity threatened her frail frame. The mounds of hair she would malt quicker than I could sweep are a thing of the past. All that is left are a few rust stains on the floor, a result of placing the cage on top of a freshly mopped floor far too many times.

On Wednesday, August 8, 2012, I took my dog Habit to the veterinarian for the last time. Her back left hip had gotten so weak that she was walking with her butt at a 90-degree angle; she was falling at least a dozen times a night and would howl in pain until I rushed to her side to pick her up and comfort her; she could no longer eat an entire bowl of food without toppling over, often found lying on the floor with her face in the bowl, desperately trying to reach her meal; she couldn't go on walks at all; and I would sometimes find her in the morning lying in her own feces, as she lost control of her bladder months ago.

I had been wrestling with the decision for months. And on Tuesday night – a particularly painful night for her – I laid next to her throw rug as she moaned in pain, I stroked her head and I told her that this was our last night together. I could not put it off anymore. I did not even want to take a day or two to shower her with attention so she could have a grand sendoff; I knew if she had one good day in which she did not fall or get hurt, I would talk myself out of it and she would spend another few months in pain.

While part of me will naturally always wonder if I made the right decision, most of me knows that I did.

Regardless, as I write this a few days after her "passing," I have yet to go one hour since her death at 10:07 a.m. on that sad Wednesday without either breaking down in tears or fighting off tears.

I am miserable. I miss my best friend. My god do I miss her. She has been with me through thick and thin for 15 ½ of her 19 years. I don't think I have ever taken a death this hard. That fact has confused me. Does it make me cold to humans that a dog meant more to me than the three close friends of mine who have died young or my closest uncle who died while only in his 60s or all of my four grandparents? After days of soul searching, I realized that the reason the death of Habit is so painful is that it is the first death with which I have dealt that the deceased relied on me. I was supposed to protect her. Instead, I was the one who drove her to be "put to sleep." Her last memory of the person she loved more than anything else in this world, the person who was supposed to look out for her, was him allowing a stranger to inject her with death.

Friends and family have reminded that I made the right decision and that in time I will come to grips that there was no other alternative. Everyone has told me that the haunting memory of the light leaving her eyes will be replaced with memories of the good times we shared. But I don't want the memory of her death to go away. I won't let it. I don't deserve reprieve from this pain. I deserve to be punished. Not because I took her to be killed, but because I abandoned her a year ago. The last year of her life was one of misery.

After Ben was born and we opened The Buzz, I could not find time for Habit. I could not find a way to juggle life in a way that allowed me even an hour a day with her. My desk in her room became muddled with files from my writing jobs, so cluttered that I couldn't work back there anymore; I had NO time to sort through everything. And without the necessary walks possible because of her declining hips, I had no reason to HAVE to spend time with her … so she was pushed to the background of my life.

In my single days my parents liked to laugh that they had never seen a dog so attached to their owner as Habit was to me. If I was home, she was next to me – either on the couch, in my bed or following my every step as I strolled around my residence. She would not leave my side … until I forced her to. She loved me so much that she would have followed me around 24 hours a day if I allowed her. And in the end, I would not allow her to spend time with me.

I often imagined her in her room at night, crying in her mind, wondering why I did not love her anymore. The thought would drive me insane and into tears and I would promise myself that I would find a way to see her more, but I could never find that balance.

In the weeks before I "put her to sleep," a plan was in the works. I was cleaning and clearing out her room and turning it back into an office so I could work from there at night and on the days when Amy has off and takes care of Ben. I am currently typing this from the desk in that room. I was just days away from finishing when she was "put to sleep." If she could have lasted a few more months, perhaps my mindset would have been different. But I could not keep her alive and in pain to appease my own conscience.

On the way to the vet that dreadful morning, she stretched across the passenger seat and placed her head in my lap. I took one hand off the wheel and stroked her head. She purred as I did it. She had no idea I was taking her to her death. In her mind, she was happier than she had been in a year – I was spending time with her just as I once did. In her mind, I loved her more than anything else in the world again; she was my number one, not my number five.

While we sat on the floor in the room in the vet's office where she would be "put to sleep," she continued to moan in delight as I scratched her ears. And when we placed her on the table so the vet could inject her with the poison, she was happy until the end as I continued to pet her. I don't take solace in this, however. While it could be argued that her last memory was that I loved her, I cannot see it that way. I keep imagining that she was thinking that, "He loves me AGAIN" ... and then ... her soul was snatched from her body because I made the decision that it was time.

I sat in the that room alone for 10 minutes sobbing and kissing her ... no, I didn't so much kiss her as I sucked on her head and cried out that I loved her and was so sorry for being so bad to her this past year. I begged her corpse for forgiveness.

As I drove home, I decided I don't deserve her forgiveness yet.

And I will never forgive myself for abandoning her as I did this last year. I deserve to wallow in pain until the day I die.

I abandoned my dog.

She loved me so much and I abandoned her.

God I miss her.

Life is ironic.

The day she died was the anniversary of the day we arrived in Tampa; on August 8, 1999, our moving van pulled into the parking lot of The Cove apartments in South Tampa to start a new life. And on that day in 2012, I took her life.

I miss you Habit. I don't expect you to ever forgive me for the man I became in the past year ... but I hope you know that I love you so much and I miss you every second of the day.

I pray dogs do indeed go to heaven. I pray you will meet me at the gate. And if you do, I promise I will find time for you. I promise.

8/17/12
Don't Stop Believing

Amy and I recently made the dumbest decision of our relationship – we tried to take the kids to an event created for single people.

The Red Bull Wake Open came to downtown Tampa a few weeks ago. Just a few steps outside The Buzz's front door, the nation's best wakeboarders showed off their skills. It sounded like fun. It sounded cool. It sounded like a great way to spend a beautiful

Saturday. It sounded too good to be true ... it was. We lasted all of five minutes at the event before it became apparent that it would be more trouble than it was worth. Ben refused to allow us to hold him, but whenever we put him down he clumsily ran full speed toward the easy-to-slip-through-railing separating us from a 10-foot drop into the water. And the other two children complained that they were hot, thirsty, hungry, angry with Obamacare and a plethora of other things about which kids always seem to whine.

As we walked back to our car, Amy and I gazed longingly at all the single 20- and 30-somethings passing us. The only baggage they carried was that day's alcohol supply. They hadn't a worry in the world. They didn't even care if they could see the event. They were not there for the wakeboarders. It was just an excuse to drink.

"Do you ever regret it," asked Amy. Most men get used to being settled down with a girlfriend and then a wife, she explained, as they adjust to "prison life." If it is the life for them, they then get to test the family waters with one child and if they don't like the path toward no freedom to which it is leading, they can stop having children and enjoy the relative freedom that one child still offers. I, on the other hand, never had time to test the waters, she reminded me. One day I was free from responsibility. The next day I had a mountain of responsibility on my plate.

Me? Regret? Am I the type of man who would have regret? OF COURSE! I am human after all and all humans are plagued from birth with the dreaded "The Grass Is Always Greener Disease."

I believe that most men and women who start families late in life have a level of regret when life gets complicated – when the kids start screaming, when the bills pile up, when all you want is five seconds to catch your breath but can only get .05 seconds. (Those who start families young may have some moments of regret as well, but I cannot speak from experience.) Longtime single people grew accustomed to peaceful lives. I often heard that when men and women hit their mid-30s, if they are not yet settled down it is hard to do so because they are so set on their calm and peaceful boat that the slightest wave rattles them. Kids are not waves. They are tsunamis to a longtime single person and I have THREE wreaking havoc on my canoe.

My few moments of regret have never revolved around bars,

partying and women, as most people would think. My moments of regret always revolve around time and money. I have to take on more work than ever before because I now have three kids. Yet, ironically, I have never had less money saved and I have never had less time to work. It gets stressful.

We all have our moments when we believe that the grass is greener. It is natural to think that life would have been better if we had made other decisions – We want so badly to move but when we do we miss our old home and forget all of its downfalls that made our lives miserable; we want to change careers because we are miserable but when we do we miss the old one; we want to change hairstyles but when we do we think we looked better with the old one (I know, I am bald, but I do remember what it was like to have hair), and so on. We all strive for change and to better ourselves but when we do the uncertainty of a new future causes us to desire our past because the past is always certain. We forget that the past would also have led to an uncertain future.

With all that said, Amy's ex-in-laws were in town last week and they took their two grandchildren to a resort for a few days. It was the first time I have been away from the two older children for more than a few hours since we all moved in together. Then, my parents came to town and were able to look after Ben during the day. For the first time in a longtime I tasted pure freedom again. I could work. I could go to the gym whenever I wanted. I could even nap.

I was miserable.

I missed the older kids. I missed Ben. I missed the stress of family life.

The grass is ALWAYS greener.

Adding to my misery was that I was worrying that the older two kids would not miss me. I knew they would miss Amy, but what if they didn't bat an eyelash at not seeing me? Would it reaffirm that they are NOT my biological kids? Ben misses me when I leave him for a second. What if they left me for days and did not care?

I was at a meeting when the kids came home. Amy sent me a text message that said the first thing the kids asked her was, "Where is dad?" I cannot remember the last time a text message made me so happy. I was smiling like a single man who just learned that a one night stand's pregnancy test came back negative! I was smiling like

The Overnight Family Man

a single man who just found out the bar across the street from him is giving away free beer! I was smiling … well … I was smiling like a man who loves his family.

As I contemplated that moment of bliss and what it meant, I concluded that. I am not an Overnight Family Man anymore. I am simply a family man. And I realized that perhaps it is time to bring this journal to an end.

Did Habit's death have anything to do with this revelation? Absolutely. I realized after her death that she was my last link to my single life. My old friends? Most of them are gone and the remaining ones I rarely see. Instead, I spend free time with my family. My longtime gym? Gone. I left it to join the Y to accommodate my family. Drunken Gasparilla days? Gone. My office? I still have it, but I work from home with Ben now. I have not seen that office in months. Every aspect of my single life is gone.

When you watch television series for a number of years, the ending is never sudden, well, except in *The Sopranos*. The characters begin coasting toward their final destinations over the course of the final two seasons or so, all culminating in an epic finale that ties everything together.

While my life is obviously real and not a TV show, I still always hoped that my journal of single man to family man would mimic such a format – that I would see the end of this journal on the horizon because I could see the changes within me slowly occurring. I hoped that I would gradually and poetically bring the journal to an epic finale. I was foolish to believe such a thing. How could my journal come to a slow end when its very premise is based upon me making such a quick and bold decision – to leave my single life behind after knowing a woman and her two kids for less than six months? My realization that I evolved into a true family man came on as quickly as my realization that I was ready to commit to a family. No matter how sudden it was, what I had to do was evident – this journal had to end because its premise is no longer relevant. I am not an overnight family man anymore.

Now that I have had time to digest the revelation, I can look back and see the changes I went through. When Amy and I first moved in together, I was overwhelmed by it all. Then I settled in and embraced the fatherly role, as evident by skipping Gasparilla my first year. Then, Ben was born and I was overwhelmed again. Then, most shockingly, not only did I settle in again but I became a stay-at-home working dad. On April 22, 2010 I was single. Today, I am a stay-at-home dad who juggles a career. Crazy.

When the kids were gone for those two days and my life was quiet again, I was lonely. I was never lonely when I was single and without a wife or kids, but now I would be miserable without them. The truth is, if tomorrow I was single with no kids, I would have a harder time coping with that than I did when I first became a family man.

Of course I will always have regret. I have regret revolving around everything I do – from my career choice to what I ate for dinner the other day. But those regrets are only momentary. Whenever I have time to think, I realize I have made the right choices – I was born to be a writer and the pizza, while unhealthy, was delicious.

My moments of regret revolving around my family life will never manifest in me attempting to run back to the single life as many stupid and selfish family men have done. I will always have my grass is greener moments, but deep down inside I know that the grass will never be any greener than it is when I am with my family.

The Overnight Family Man is dead. A little over two years ago I was single and unprepared for a family. Today, I am a father of three.

I will never pretend to be father of the year. I have plenty of flaws. However, I think all of those flaws are outweighed by the by largest attribute – I love my kids more than anything else on the planet. And that is what separates a Family Man in training from a real Family Man.

Would I still try a magical sex rock? Of course. However, I cannot picture Amy and I ever having enough alone time to warrant its power.

The story of the Overnight Family Man is complete.

Cue Journey's "Don't Stop Believing" and cut suddenly to black

About the Author

Paul Guzzo had been a journalist in the Tampa Bay area since 1999. He has written for close to two dozen publications, including *La Gaceta Newspaper* and *Tampa Bay Parenting*, both for which he pens parenting columns. Along with his brother, Pete, he is also an award-winning independent filmmaker.

www.ingramcontent.com/pod-product-compliance
Lightning Source LLC
Chambersburg PA
CBHW071710090426
42738CB00009B/1733